Intelligent Guides to Wi

MW00939954

Chablis

2020 Edition

Wines of Chablis

Benjamin Lewin MW

Copyright © 2017, 2018, 2019, 2020 Benjamin Lewin

ISBN: 9781980656890

Vendange Press

www.vendangepress.com

Preface

This Guide is devoted to Chablis. Two other guides cover other parts of Burgundy: the *Guide to Burgundy: Côte d'Or*, and the *Guide to Southern Burgundy*, which focuses on the Côte Chalonnaise and Mâcon, as well as Beaujolais and Jura-Savoie.

The first part of the guide discusses the regions, and explains the character and range of the wines. The second part profiles the producers. There are detailed profiles of the leading producers, showing how each winemaker interprets the local character, and mini-profiles of other important estates.

In the first part, I address the nature of the wines made today and ask how this has changed, how it's driven by tradition or competition, and how styles may evolve in the future. I show how the wines are related to the terroir and to the types of grape varieties that are grown, and I explain the classification system. For each region, I suggest reference wines that illustrate the character and variety of the area.

In the second part, there's no single definition for what constitutes a top producer. Leading producers range from those who are so prominent as to represent the common public face of an appellation to those who demonstrate an unexpected potential on a tiny scale. The producers profiled in the guide represent the best of both tradition and innovation in wine in the region. In each profile, I have tried to give a sense of the producer's aims for his wines, of the personality and philosophy behind them—to meet the person who makes the wine, as it were, as much as to review the wines themselves.

Each profile shows a sample label, a picture of the winery, and details of production, followed by a description of the producer and winemaker. Each producer is rated (from one to four stars). For each producer I suggest reference wines that are a good starting point for understanding the style. Most of the producers welcome visits, although some require appointments: details are in the profiles. Profiles are organized geographically, and are preceded by maps showing the locations of producers to help plan itineraries.

The guide is based on many visits to the region over recent years. I owe an enormous debt to the many producers who cooperated in this venture by engaging in discussion and opening innumerable bottles for tasting. This guide would not have been possible without them.

Benjamin Lewin

Contents

Overview of Burgundy   1

Chablis and Limestone   3

The Chablis AOP   5

Grand Crus   6

Premier Crus   7

Styles of Chablis   10

Oak in Chablis   12

Longevity of Chablis   16

Visiting the Region   16

Vintages   18

Maps   20

Profiles of Leading Estates   22

Mini-Profiles of Important Estates   64

Glossary of French Wine Terms   73

Index of Estates by Rating   76

Index of Organic and Biodynamic Estates   77

Index of Estates by Name   78

Tables

Premier Crus   9

Reference Wines for Chablis   15

Appellation Maps

Appellations in the Kimmeridgian Chain   4

The Grand Crus   6

The Premier Crus   8

Producer Maps

Chablis AOP   20

Town of Chablis   21

Symbols for Producers   22

Overview of Burgundy

Chablis is the northwestern outpost of Burgundy, which stretches all the way to Beaujolais, a hundred and fifty miles to the south. Production in Burgundy overall is around two thirds white, with the major regions for white wine being Chablis, the Côte de Beaune, and the Mâconnais. Each has a distinct style. Almost all the white wine is 100% Chardonnay. There is a little Aligoté in generic Bourgogne.

Because of its cooler climate, Chablis today is thought of as a crisper, more mineral wine than Côte d'Or, but historically the difference was not so obvious. In the fourteenth century, wine from Auxerre (just to the west of Chablis) sold at a higher price than wine from Beaune. Before phylloxera, in fact, Auxerre was close to a monoculture of vines, but it never recovered from the loss of the vineyards. Chablis is essentially what remains. Just to the southwest, the tiny AOP of Sauvignon St. Bris is the one place in Burgundy where Sauvignon Blanc is allowed, and adjacent to it lies Irancy AOP, where Pinot Noir is grown. Some Chablis producers also have small vineyards in these appellations. Chablis was very much a minor region until recently, but with around 5,000 ha today, it's comparable to the Côte de Beaune.

Burgundy is famous for its highly hierarchical appellation system, based on the view that the potential of every vineyard is different. The classification system is organized into a relatively steep pyramid, steadily narrowing from the base of two thirds of regional AOPs, to a quarter in village appellations, with 11% of premier crus and 1.4% of grand crus at the peak.

At the base of the pyramid, generic Bourgogne AOPs can come from anywhere in the entire region of Burgundy. This includes a very wide range of wines, extending from those including Gamay and Aligoté to those coming from Pinot Noir or Chardonnay from just outside the borders of famous villages. The name of the producer is the only guide to the potential quality of Bourgogne AOP.

Being part of Burgundy, Chablis has a similar hierarchical system, although not so detailed since Chablis is a single commune. In ascending order, the levels are Petit Chablis, Chablis, Premier Cru, and Grand Cru. The only grape grown in Chablis is Chardonnay. Chablis accounts for 20% of production in the region of Burgundy.

2

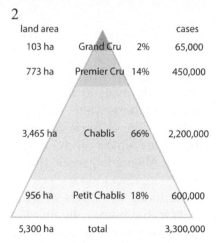

land area			cases
103 ha	Grand Cru	2%	65,000
773 ha	Premier Cru	14%	450,000
3,465 ha	Chablis	66%	2,200,000
956 ha	Petit Chablis	18%	600,000
5,300 ha	total		3,300,000

Chablis AOP is more than half of production.

Like the rest of Burgundy, individual vineyard holdings are quite small. Most producers have a range of wines, from Petit Chablis and Chablis to premier and grand crus. A typical producer probably makes 6-10 different wines.

Before the French Revolution, most vineyards were owned by the Church or large landowners. After they were confiscated as "biens nationaux," they became subdivided. The situation has since been exacerbated by French inheritance law, which requires that an estate must be split equally between all the heirs. Today most premier and grand crus are divided between multiple owners. Clos Vougeot's 50 hectares are distributed among roughly 80 growers; the largest has only 5.5 ha, and the smallest has only a few rows of vines. The same is true of Chablis: there are just over 100 ha of grand cru vineyards, but they are divided among (probably) around a hundred growers, with more than 60 producers making grand cru Chablis.

The major part of production in Burgundy comes from negociants, followed by cooperatives, with independent growers as the smallest category. In Chablis there are 23 negociants and 353 individual growers. Many growers belong to a cooperative; cooperatives account for a quarter of production. Some of the important negociants in Burgundy own estates in Chablis; Joseph Drouhin owns Drouhin-Vaudon, Louis Latour owns Simonnet-Febvre, and Faiveley owns Billaud-Simon.

The label may indicate whether a wine comes from a domain or negociant as the word "Domaine" can be used only for estate-grown grapes, whereas "Maison" indicates that they come from a negociant activity. Some producers who undertake both activities distinguish between them by different labels; others don't use either Domaine or Maison, and make no distinction.

Chablis and Limestone

Chablis stands alone from the rest of Burgundy, both geographically and psychologically. Well to the north, it has the most marginal climate; ripening has traditionally been a problem. It's been the epitome of minerality in white wine, traditionally very different from the fleshiness of the Côte d'Or. Its distinctive geology is based on the famous Kimmeridgian limestone, a soft mixture of clay and limestone, generally gray in color. This was laid down when the sea retreated in the Jurassic period, leaving a bed of fossils that give the soil its calcareous nature. (Several producers have large fossils, retrieved from their vineyards, on show in their tasting rooms.)

A stretch of limestone, the Kimmeridgian chain, runs from Sancerre, through Chablis, to the southernmost part of Champagne. It is history and climate that focus on Sauvignon Blanc in Sancerre, Chardonnay in Chablis, and sparkling wine in Champagne. (Premier Cru Mont de Milieu in Chablis supposedly takes its name for being halfway between Champagne and Burgundy.)

Kimmeridgian limestone occupies about half of the Chablis region; the rest consists of Portlandian limestone, harder in structure and browner in color. When the AOC was defined, the area for Chablis and its premier and grand crus was restricted to vineyards on Kimmeridgian soil. There was not much doubt that the quality dropped on leaving Kimmeridgian terroir. Portlandian limestone was restricted to the lowest level, Petit Chablis.

Was the superiority of Kimmeridgian limestone due only to the soil? The Kimmeridgian soil is located on the south and east-facing slopes, where good exposure helps to compensate for the cool climate, whereas the harder Portlandian soil occupies the plateaus at higher elevations (where the grapes are slower to ripen). The original distinction was not ill-founded, but it had more to do with aspect and slope than with the underlying geology.

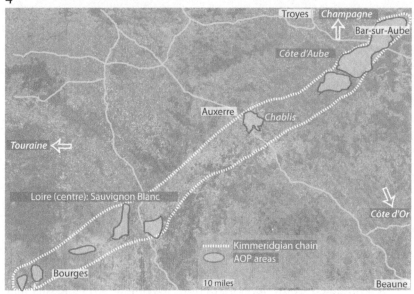

The vineyards of Chablis are in the middle of the Kimmeridgian chain. Chardonnay is also grown to the northeast for the Aube area of Champagne. Sauvignon Blanc is grown to the southwest in the Loire.

When the Chablis AOC was defined in 1938, the total vineyard area was only 400 ha. Restricting Chablis and its premier and grand crus to Kimmeridgian limestone continued to be the case as the AOC expanded to include vineyards in communes around Chablis. But in 1978, when a further expansion occurred, the restriction was dropped. It's hard to better producer William Fèvre's protest at the time: "These areas of woodland and scrub have never had Chardonnay vines in the past. When these bounds are passed, there are no longer any limits."

The Chablis AOP

Chablis comes from both banks of the river Serein, extending away from the town. Petit Chablis comes from outlying areas (the best Petit Chablis tend to come from the plateau above the grand crus). The most important vineyards are near the town. The premier crus are not quite as numerous as they might seem from the variety of labels—there are 40 different names altogether—because many have separate names for different *climats* within them. Just opposite the town on the right bank, a long curve of vineyards is divided into seven Grand Cru *climats*.

Coming from a cool climate (often marginal until the recent warming trend), Chablis traditionally has crisp acidity. Petit Chablis has greatly benefited from warmer vintages, and the best Petit Chablis today is close to the quality of Chablis twenty or so years ago. There is always good acidity, but the wine can be quite fruity and very agreeable for drinking immediately.

The main difference in going to Chablis AOP is a sense of greater fruit density on the palate, with more texture and flavor variety. Chablis AOP is intended for drinking soon after release; it is a rare cuvée that benefits from being held for more than three years.

Premier crus show the greatest range of quality, from those that are barely distinguishable from a top communal wine in a good year, to those that skirt the quality of the grand crus. Alcohol is more moderate than on the Côte d'Or, usually 12.5% for communal Chablis, often 13% for the premier crus and usually 13% for the grand crus, but rarely more than 13%. "If you harvest at more than 13% alcohol you make Chardonnay not Chablis. If we harvested by the same criteria as 20-30 years ago, we would have a great increase in alcohol, but now we harvest 2-3 weeks earlier to keep freshness and avoid it," says Benoît Droin.

Once you leave the grand crus and top premier crus behind, Chablis is a good deal less interesting. It's certainly worth paying the (relatively) modest premium for a premier cru compared to communal Chablis.

Like all Burgundy, the producer's name is of paramount importance, and negociants have generally been well in second place behind individual growers. There are some important exceptions. Verget (based in Mâcon) was viewed with suspicion for producing Chablis in a richer style twenty years ago. More recently, Patrick Piuze and Benjamin Laroche (La Manufacture) have adopted a micro-negociant model, being involved in grape-growing of specific plots, and making wine to their own specifications.

The major cooperative in Chablis, La Chablisienne, is unusually important, one of the most respected in the country; and because it represents many small growers, offers the widest range of wines (in fact, probably the only opportunity to compare the entire range of crus).

Grand Crus

The grand crus occupy a continuous slope, but the land folds and turns so there are changes in exposure and slope, with significant variation in character. Technically there is one Chablis grand cru, with seven *climats*, but in practice these are regarded as though there were seven different grand crus.

The grand crus extend all the way from the road just on the edge of the town to the woods at the top of the hill. With the much slighter slope along the Côte de Nuits, for example, everything depends on position on the slope, but no distinction is made within Chablis grand crus, even though there are differences in soil types

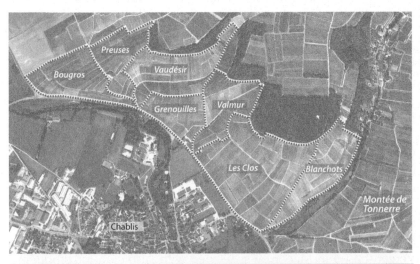

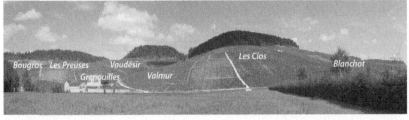

The grand crus form a single continuous line of vineyards with varying slopes and exposures. (Premier Cru Montée de Tonnerre lies across a gully at the end of the slope.

as well as exposure to the sun. As a general rule, the grand crus tend to be more directly south-facing than the premier crus—this is part of their advantage—but there are sufficient twists and turns in the land that it's not a hard and fast rule.

Les Clos, the largest grand cru, always makes the most powerful wine, irrespective of whether the plot is in a protected position under the trees at the top or exposed in the middle or at the bottom. The minerality of Chablis reaches its peak in Les Clos. Whenever a producer has more than one grand cru, the Les Clos stands out for its reserve when young, which translates into greater longevity.

Valmur is usually richer and less mineral; Vaudésir has an intensity that can border on spicy. Les Preuses has more of a perfumed delicacy; Blanchots can be delicate also; and Grenouilles, at the foot of the slope, is firmer; while Bougros is considered to be the slightest of the grand crus.

Premier Crus

There are three premier crus on the right bank: Fourchaume is just to the north; Montée de Tonnerre (the premier cru that most often approaches the grand crus in quality) is across a deep gully just to the south, and Mont de Milieu is parallel to it farther south.

On the left bank, Chablis is really a series of valleys, fanning out from the town. As there are vineyards on both sides of the valleys, they face in all directions. Usually the premier crus are the most south facing. Montmains and Vaillons, which are the best premier crus on the left bank, have similar southeast exposures on parallel hillsides in adjacent valleys, as does Côte de Léchet.

Usually in Burgundy there's a fine line between premier crus and grand crus, with some premier crus standing out above the others and occasioning argument as to whether they should be promoted to grand cru. In Chablis the argument is more at the other end: there is doubt whether some of the premier crus created in 1978 merit the description.

There are certainly far too many premier crus, or to be more precise, too many overlapping names within the premier crus. This can make it more difficult for a premier cru to establish a clear impression. A handful of the *climats* within the premier crus are well

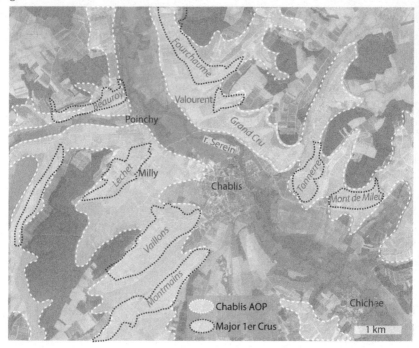

The grand crus face the town of Chablis. The best premier crus are in line with the grand crus or immediately across the river.

known, mostly because they used by top producers, such as Valourent (in Fourchaume), Chapelot (in Montée de Tonnerre), La Fôret and Butteaux (in Montmains) or Séchets (in Vaillons), but for the most part they are more like brand names than useful descriptions of origin.

It is not straightforward to find a defining difference between the premier crus of the left and right banks, but perhaps it is fair to say that the left bank crus tend to be more linear, more mineral, and to show more salinity; while on the right bank, Mont de Milieu and Montée de Tonnerre, and especially Fourchaume, have more fat, more weight on the palate.

It is also true that the right bank premier crus are all long established as adjuncts to the grand crus, but the impression of left bank premier crus is somewhat diluted by the "new" premier crus (created in 1978), which vary from approaching the quality of the original premier crus to barely above appellation standard.

Premier Cru	Climats
Chablis has 17 premier crus but a total of 89 individual climats	
Right Bank	
Fourchaume	Côte de Fontenay, L'Homme Mort, Vaulorent, Vaupulent
Vaucoupin	
Montée de Tonnerre	Chapelot, Pied d'Aloup, Côte de Bréchain
Mont de Milieu	
Left Bank	
Beauroy	Côte de Savant, Troesmes
Berdiot	
Les Beauregards	Côte de Cuisy
Chaume de Talvat	
Côte de Jouan	
Côte de Léchet	
Côte de Vaubarousse	
Les Fourneaux	Morein, Côte des Près Girots
Montmains	Forêts, Butteaux
Vaillons	Beugnons, Chatains, les Épinottes, Les Lys, Mélinots, Roncières, Séchets
Vaudevey	Vaux Ragons
Vauligneau	Vau de Longue, Vau Girault, La Forêt, Sur la Forêt
Vosgros	Vaugiraut

The most important premier crus are shown in bold. The most commonly found climats for each premier cru are shown on the right.

Styles of Chablis

"They were all so bad in Chablis twenty years ago. For me, concentration is important, lower yields and riper. But everyone said, we are making Chablis, it's never ripe, the typical Chablis is green. People said, when you make ripe Chablis, it loses its character. But you can't make wine from unripe grapes—all green wines taste the same," says negociant Jean-Marie Guffens, who makes a wide range of Chablis at Verget. Today the rest of Chablis has caught up, and that increase in ripeness is typical of the entire appellation. If effects of global warming on white wine are evident anywhere in Burgundy, it's in Chablis.

The first time I tasted a Chablis from Verget, I was certainly surprised: its density and fatness of structure were quite unusual. It seemed to mark a move in the direction of the Côte d'Or. Jean-Marie's view, of course, would be that instead of surrendering to a traditional view that Chablis is inevitably thin and acid, he was bringing out the true potential of the region. Today this would not be so surprising: in vintages such as 2002, 2005, 2009, or 2015, many Chablis at premier or grand cru level have moved towards the richer style of the Côte d'Or. (Of course, the whites of the Côte d'Or have also become richer.)

"Global warming has been beneficial for Chablis. My father would have been the happiest of men with the quality of the poorest years we had in the past decade," says Bernard Raveneau of Domaine François Raveneau. Didier Seguier at William Fèvre thinks global warming is a great opportunity, giving better wines that retain acidity and balance, but without losing character. "The typicity of our wine comes from the Kimmeridgian terroir, it's very different (from the Côte d'Or). Warming gives a very interesting maturity today but not sur-maturity."

At one of the domains that has stayed true to the traditions of Chablis right through the era of global warming, Bernard Raveneau expressed an interesting view of the difference between Chablis and the Côte d'Or when I asked why Chablis does seem to have had the same problems with premox (premature oxidation) as white Burgundy. "We haven't been following some of the trends of the Côte d'Or such as excessive battonage or reduction of sulfur. On the

Côte d'Or they are very traditional, here in Chablis we are more modern, oenological techniques are more evident, it's a different mentality. People in Chablis pay more attention to winemaking; on Cote d'Or, if malo doesn't start, they'll shrug and wait until the Spring when it warms up, here people will do something about it, to get the process finished. Chablis is the New World of Burgundy. In the 1960s, Chablis was 700 ha, today it's 5,500 ha—so it's a very new vineyard and people are more modern, they like investing in technology, where in Côte d'Or it's very ancestral."

When I ask producers how they see Chablis today, the answers are pretty uniform: it should retain freshness and minerality. Following up by asking how its character has changed, the answer is generally dismissive: it hasn't really changed at all, they say. Global warming has been beneficial; chaptalization has become rare, difficult vintages have turned out much better than they used to, but that essential tension between fruit and acidity, perhaps what the French call nervosité, hasn't changed at all. I don't agree on this last, crucial point about character.

I remember when most Chablis was thin and acid, where the fruits (if you could detect them) were bitter lemon or grapefruit. Granted that citrus remains the dominant flavor in the Chablis spectrum, often enough today it moves from fresh citrus to stewed fruits, rounder and softer, and often enough there are notes of stone fruits running in the direction of peaches or even apricots. Minerality is hard to describe, but like pornography you know it when you taste it, and it's fair in my opinion to say that in many cases it has now become subservient to the fruits.

Climate change has certainly had a significant effect in Chablis. While the effects have mostly been beneficial, there has also been collateral damage in the form of more erratic weather patterns, especially in the crucial period of the Spring. Freezing weather in April dramatically reduced the crop in 2016 and 2017, even hitting areas that usually have been exempt. Hailstorms have become more of an occupational hazard, to the point at which INAO finally relented and allowed hail nets to be used as of 2018. But the general drift of these problems is that they reduce quantity, and the wine that is made is good quality. Like other marginal wine regions, the balance has shifted from a minotiry of really good vintages each decade to a minority of poor vintages.

Oak in Chablis

The big divide in Chablis used to be between producers who do or do not use oak. "In the eighties there were two big schools, cuve and oak; my father was always stainless steel; he used to say, I'm not in the timber business. But he has changed his mind," says Fabien Moreau at Christian Moreau. "William Fèvre always used some new oak, but that stopped as soon as Henriot took over in 1998. We didn't want to *boisé* the vin, to the contrary we wanted to keep freshness," says Didier Seguier, who came to Fèvre from Bouchard at the time. Here you see the convergence in Chablis: protagonists for stainless steel have taken up oak, while protagonists for oak have backed off.

Richer vintages may be partly responsible for the convergence of style. Many producers now use a mixture of maturation in cuve and barrique. Where partial oak is used, the wine may spend only six months in oak before assemblage with the wine from cuve, after which it spends another six months in cuve only.

Two producers stand out in the oak camp: François Raveneau and Vincent Dauvissat are generally recognized as the best in Chablis. But neither uses any new oak. Each house is notable for the subtlety of its style. Is global warming a threat to that subtlety? "No, personally I think the place will adjust. I harvest early, the terroir resets the balance, it's the backbone of the wine," says Vincent Dauvissat.

Minerality is always there as a thread running from nose through palate to finish, fruits tend to the citrus spectrum but with hints of stone fruits more evident in warmer vintages, and there's a delicious overtone of anise or liquorice on the finish. Les Clos is the epitome of the style for both producers, always showing a more evident streak of structure, with Valmur placing second for Raveneau, and Les Preuses second for Dauvissat. Montée de Tonnerre is the best of the premier crus for both.

Other producers in the oak camp have their own styles. At Jean-Paul and Benoît Droin, the style is richer, and the various crus have different maturation regimes. Stainless steel is used for Chablis AOP, some premier crus, and Blanchots, but Mont de Milieu and Montée de Tonnerre have 25% oak, which increases to 35% for Vaudésir, 40% for Montmains and Valmur, and 50% for Fourchaume and Les

Clos. The interesting feature is that there isn't a straight increase going from premier crus to grand crus, as would be usual in the Côte d'Or, but a view that different terroirs have different potentials for handling oak. There is a little new oak here, but less than there used to be, now limited to no more than 10% in the grand crus.

The arch exponent of the unoaked style is Louis Michel, whose premier and grand crus often achieve a complexity creating the impression in blind tasting that they must have been matured in oak. But the use of barriques stopped forty years ago; since then the wines have been vinified exclusively in stainless steel. In fact, the texture and structure are due to slow fermentation followed by time on the lees (typically 6 months for Chablis, 12 months for premier cru, and 18 months for grand cru). The top wines have an almost granular texture supporting what is perhaps more a sense of steel and stone than overt minerality. They are great wines, although I don't think they have quite the same longevity as the oaked style.

Each producer has his own view on how best to express terroir differences in Chablis. Is this done by vinifying all wines in the same way, so that the only significant difference is the terroir? This is the view of both Dauvissat and Raveneau (with only oak) and Louis Michel (with only steel), and Jean-Claude Bessin (all premier and grand crus with 60% oak). Or should vinification be adjusted to the Cru, as it is at William Fèvre, Droin, Laroche, Long-Depaquit, Christian Moreau, and La Manufacture, with a general policy of increasing oak proportion going up a hierarchy of premier and grand crus. Somewhere in between are Pinson and the Chablisienne cooperative, where all premier crus get the same treatment, but grand crus get more oak.

Unlike the Côte d'Or, where all wines age in oak, and the progression from communal wine to premier cru to grand cru usually involves increasing the proportion of new oak, in Chablis the progress is more a matter of adjusting the mix of stainless steel to old oak. While many producers are committed to stainless steel and a few are committed to barriques, most of those producers who use barriques use them only partially. Lots matured in stainless steel are blended with lots matured in barrique, and there is a rough correlation between the quality of the terroir and the proportion matured in barrique, increasing through the premier crus to the grand crus.

14

François Raveneau
Vincent Dauvissat
Laurent Tribut
Pattes Loups
Jean-Claude Bessin
Louis Michel
Domaine Pinson
Samuel Billaud
William Fèvre
Christian Moreau
Billaud-Simon
Domaine Droin
Gilbert Picq
Patrick Piuze
Maison Verget
Jean Collet
Daniel Dampt
Jean Dauvissat
Drouhin-Vaudon
La Chablisienne
Nathalie et Gilles Fèvre
La Manufacture
Domaine des Malandes
Denis Race
Jean-Marc Brocard
Simonnet-Febvre
Domain Grossot
Domaine Laroche
Domaine Servin
Long-Depaquit
Verget
Garnier

SAVORY

FRUITY

A classification of producers on a scale from savory to fruity.

As a rough measure, it seems to me that producers can be classified on savory/fruity balance. The most savory would be Raveneau and Dauvissat, both committed to oak, and perhaps for that reason my favorites. But there is no exact correlation between use of oak and tendency to savory. The balance changes with every cuvée and vintage, of course, but perhaps this is a useful guide to thinking about how producers fit into changing styles. The differences are not as violent as the arguments in some other locations between modernists and traditionalists, but the fruity style may be more modern, at least in the sense that wines like this would have been difficult or impossible to produce until recent times.

Reference Wines for Chablis	
Petit Chablis	L. C. Poitout Domaine Vrignaud
Chablis	Jean-Claude Bessin Samuel Billaud Gilbert Picq (Vieilles Vignes)
Premier Crus	
Fourchaume	William Fèvre Nathalie & Gilles Fèvre
L'Homme Mort	Domaine de Chantermerle (Francis Boudin)
Mont de Milieu	Louis Pinson Jean Collet et Fils
Montmains	Domaine Laroche Laurent Tribut
Montée de Tonnerre	Jean-Paul et Benoît Droin Louis Michel
Vaillons	Christian Moreau Louis Moreau La Manufacture
Grand Crus	
Blanchots	Domaine Laroche
Bougros	William Fèvre
Grenouilles	La Chablisienne
Preuses	Vincent Dauvissat William Fèvre
Vaudésir	Billaud Simon Louis Michel
Valmur	François Raveneau Jean-Paul et Benoît Droin
Les Clos	François Raveneau Vincent Dauvissat

The Longevity of Chablis

The great issue of the day in white Burgundy crosses all appellation boundaries. This is premature oxidation, so prevalent today that it has become known by the abbreviation of premox. The problem first became widely apparent with the 1996 vintage, when soon after 2000 many wines, even at premier cru level, began to show signs of oxidation: deepening color, a madeirized nose, and drying out on the palate. My impression is that the problem is worse in the richer vintages (which previously would have been expected to be the more long lived). Fitting with that view, Chablis suffers less than whites from the Côte d'Or.

I wonder whether a difference is battonage is a contributing factor to the occurrence of premature oxidation on the Côte d'Or and its relative absence in Chablis. Named for the wooden baton that used to be used, battonage stirs up the lees periodically to increase richness in the wine. Although maturation on the lees is common, typically for around 12 months for premier cru and around 18 months for grand cru, battonage is unusual in Chablis. "We don't have the same body and strength as the Cote de Beaune, if we go too far with battonage the wine will be good at first but will tire quickly," says Sandrine Audegond at Domaine Laroche.

Premox is not a problem with Petit Chablis or Chablis anyway, as they are intended to be enjoyed young: I would drink Petit Chablis immediately and would not keep a Chablis AOP for more than a couple of years. The best premier crus—Montée de Tonnerre, Fourchaume, Mont de Milieu, Vaillons, Montmains—from a good producer should improve over four or five years; premier crus from Raveneau or Dauvissat will last for around a decade. Grand Crus really should not really be started until five or six years after the vintage and should last for a decade. Les Clos is the longest lived of all; it can even be on the austere side when young.

Visiting the Region

Chablis is a tiny area. Many producers are located in the town itself, and it's possible to walk from one to the next. Many whose addresses are in Chablis are actually in small villages on the out-

Chablis is a compact town with an increased interest in tourism. Many producers are within a five minute walk of the entrance.

skirts, 5-10 minutes drive away. Staying in the town means you can easily walk to about half of the producers. Some can be visited without an appointment, but you may get a more comprehensive tasting if you make an appointment a few days or a week or so ahead.

The town of Chablis used to be something of a wasteland for tourists, but with producers moving more towards an interest in oenotourism, some now run restaurants and small hotels in the town, so the scene for tourists is much improved.

There are not many large negociants or producers, and at the smaller producers in the villages it will very likely be the owner/winemaker (more properly the vigneron) who shows you around. (This makes it a very good idea to have an appointment.) Seeing winery facilities is common, but you do not usually get taken into the vineyards. Some of the smaller producers may not speak English.

Only the larger negociants or producers have dedicated tasting rooms. At smaller producers, often enough the winery is basically an extension of the family residence. Tastings are often in the cave (take a sweater), and sometimes from barrels if bottles are considered too precious to open for visitors. Be prepared to taste samples taken from the barrel with a pipette (sometimes involving shared glasses. Most visits last around an hour. Most producers sell wine at the cellar.

The etiquette of tasting assumes you will spit. A producer will be surprised if you drink the wine. Usually a tasting room or cellar is equipped with spittoons, but ask if you do not see one (crachoir in French).

Vintages

"With climate change, the wines of Chablis have really changed, the situation is completely different from the eighties," says Vincent Dampt at Domaine Daniel Dampt. Global warming has brought the style of Chablis more into line with the rest of Burgundy, and vintages today tend to be divided into those that are characterized as classic, because the predominant influence is that fresh, lively acidity, as opposed to warmer vintages where there is palpably more richness. In warmer vintages such as 2005 and 2009, the wines have been lovely at first, but have not had their usual longevity. In 2015 the wines were attractive on release, but give the impression of retaining enough freshness to last well. "Our experience in 2009 has helped us to do better in 2015," says Vincent Dampt. "2015 is a very straightforward vintage, very facile, but Chablisiens prefer 2014 or 2016 to 2015," says Samuel Billaud.

2018	**	Warm dry summer weather as in the rest of Burgundy made for wines that are richer than usual, partly compensated by high yields, similar to 2015 but with higher dry extract. Wines are attractive when young but won't have the longevity of a truly great year.
2017	**	Freezing weather in second half of April greatly reduced yields for second year in a row. The Right Bank was badly affected, reducing production of Grand Crus and the best Premier Crus. The rest of the season was good and harvest was early, at start of September. Quality should be good.
2016	*	Difficult year in which frost, followed by mildew, and some hail, reduced crop size to around half of normal. The Left Bank (AOP Chablis and premier crus) was affected worst. The wines have that classic freshness, and the best show distinct minerality. Harvest was late at the end of September, sometimes with difficulty getting to full ripeness. They are not so immediately attractive as 2015.

2015	***	A very good, full flavored vintage. Warm year gave wines that are softer and rounder than usual, already very attractive, but perhaps not quite typical. The best will be long lived.
2014	*	Storms with hail during growing season reduced crop greatly in many communes, but weather improved after very difficult August. Wines tend to be fruity and easy, but there is good acidity. They do not have the immediate appeal of 2015.
2013		Cold growing season was difficult, but some improvement in September allowed decent harvest for wines that will be good rather than great.
2012	*	Erratic conditions led to low yields, but quality is surprisingly good, with a nice balance between fruits and acidity, and wines a little softer than usual.
2011		Difficulties in getting to ripeness make this the least successful vintage of the decade to date.
2010	***	More linear than the opulent 2009s, with an elegant balance, good acidity and minerality, and good potential for longevity. The depth of the fruits is now emerging, and the linearity is classic.
2009	***	On the rich side, sometimes over-rich, opulent at first, but unlikely to age long as richness is well ahead of acidity. Most premier and grand crus have reached their peak.
2008		Difficult vintage with problems of rain and humidity, wines on the fresh side. Acidity may be too evident for them to come around.
2007		Growing season was too wet, wines are decent but on the acid side.
2006	*	Tendency towards austerity resulted from cool conditions leading to high acidity.
2005	***	Classic opulence for a warm year, impression of fat when young, but by now the tendency to earlier aging is making most questionable.
2004		Lighter, more acid side, not many of interest today.
2003		The heat was too much, wines tended to be flabby, have not lasted.
2002	**	Initially opulent but too old now.

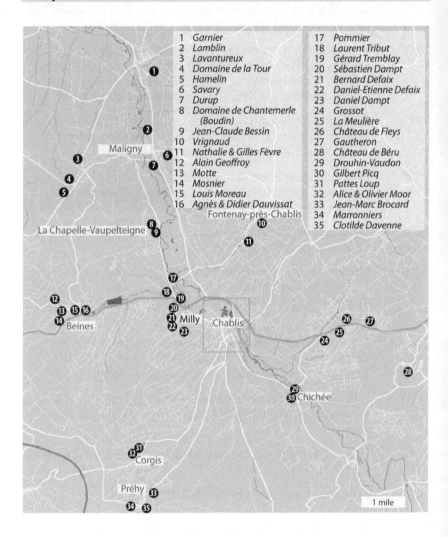

1 Garnier
2 Lamblin
3 Lavantureux
4 Domaine de la Tour
5 Hamelin
6 Savary
7 Durup
8 Domaine de Chantemerle
  (Boudin)
9 Jean-Claude Bessin
10 Vrignaud
11 Nathalie & Gilles Fèvre
12 Alain Geoffroy
13 Motte
14 Mosnier
15 Louis Moreau
16 Agnès & Didier Dauvissat

17 Pommier
18 Laurent Tribut
19 Gérard Tremblay
20 Sébastien Dampt
21 Bernard Defaix
22 Daniel-Etienne Defaix
23 Daniel Dampt
24 Grossot
25 La Meulière
26 Château de Fleys
27 Gautheron
28 Château de Béru
29 Drouhin-Vaudon
30 Gilbert Picq
31 Pattes Loup
32 Alice & Olivier Moor
33 Jean-Marc Brocard
34 Marronniers
35 Clotilde Davenne

Maligny

La Chapelle-Vaupelteigne

Fontenay-près-Chablis

Beines

Milly

Chablis

Chichée

Corgis

Préhy

1 mile

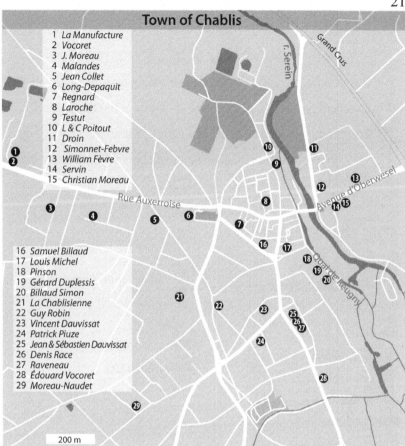

Town of Chablis

1 La Manufacture
2 Vocoret
3 J. Moreau
4 Malandes
5 Jean Collet
6 Long-Depaquit
7 Regnard
8 Laroche
9 Testut
10 L & C Poitout
11 Droin
12 Simonnet-Febvre
13 William Fèvre
14 Servin
15 Christian Moreau

16 Samuel Billaud
17 Louis Michel
18 Pinson
19 Gérard Duplessis
20 Billaud Simon
21 La Chablisienne
22 Guy Robin
23 Vincent Dauvissat
24 Patrick Piuze
25 Jean & Sébastien Dauvissat
26 Denis Race
27 Raveneau
28 Édouard Vocoret
29 Moreau-Naudet

200 m

Profiles of Leading Estates

Ratings	
****	Sui generis, standing out above everything else in the appellation
***	Excellent producers defining the very best of the appellation
**	Top producers whose wines typify the appellation
*	Very good producers making wines of character that rarely disappoint

Symbols	
⊙ *Address*	☺ *Tasting room with especially warm welcome*
☎ *Phone*	🚶 *Tastings/visits possible*
Owner/winemaker/contact	📅 *By appointment only*
@ *Email*	⊘ *No visits*
⊕ *Website*	*Sales directly at producer*
White Reference wines	*No direct sales*
Grower-producer	*Winery with accommodation*
Negociant (or purchases grapes)	
Cooperative	
Conventional viticulture	
Sustainable viticulture	
Organic	
Biodynamic	
ha=estate vineyards	
bottles=annual production	

Domaine Jean-Claude et Romain Bessin **

 Rue des Cours, 89800 La Chapelle Vaupelteigne

 (33) 03 86 42 46 77

 Evelyne & Jean-Claude Bessin

@ *dnejcbessin@wanadoo.fr*

La Forêt

 12 ha; 40,000 bottles

[map p. 20]

The domain is hidden away in the village of La Chapelle a few miles outside Chablis. Jean-Claude took over in 1992; his wife represents the sixth generation since the estate started in 1825. Estate bottling started with Jean-Claude. "My father-in-law sold all the juice to negociants. When I took over, I found it frustrating to work on the vines and vinification and sell the juice."

Most of the wine is exported. "When I started I didn't have many clients and as things developed the demand came from export, with Berry Bros in London. We just never had time to develop agents and a commercial network in France, so most is exported. I'm an artisan that's why I've never wanted to expand the domain."

Almost half the holdings are in AOP Chablis around La Chapelle: the rest are in premier and grand crus. "We don't look to increase production, we have the luck to have some vieilles vignes," Jean-Claude says. There is mixed use of wood and cuve, depending on the cuvée, and élevage lasts a year. Chablis AOP is kept in cuve with only a small proportion of barriques. Premier and grand crus are handled the same way with about 60% in barriques, using only old wood.

The style here is to bring out the minerality of the fruits. Going up the hierarchy, there is more precision, more reserve or even austerity, but increasing finesse. The single cuvée of Chablis has more character than usual for the AOP, because it comes only from old (about 60-year) vines. The Montmains has more intensity, and then La Forêt (part of Montmains, and matured only in foudre) has increased precision and minerality. Fourchaume shows more open generosity of fruits (usually there are two cuvées, one from vines of 35-45 years, the other from vines over 60 years). Valmur is relatively austere and needs more time to open out.

Domaine Samuel Billaud **

📍 *8 Boulevard du Dr Tacussel, 89800 Chablis*

📞 *(33) 03 86 51 00 07*

👤 *Samuel Billaud*

@ *samuel.billaud@orange.fr*

🌐 *samuel-billaud.com*

🍾 *Mont de Milieu*

4 ha; 60,000 bottles   [map p. 21]

"I worked for a long time at Domaine Billaud-Simon, and left in 2014 when they decided to sell the domain. I bought these premises from Moreau-Naudet in 2015," says Samuel Billaud. His new domain is set up right under the ramparts of Chablis in a group of medieval buildings around a courtyard. The buildings have been stylishly modernized inside, and there's a chic tasting room. The cuverie is full of stainless steel tanks, with many small sizes to allow vinification by parcel. In spite of the youth of the domain, there is a wide range of cuvées, including five premier crus and three grand crus.

Petit Chablis comes from an area above Les Clos. Chablis is a blend from three plots. There's also a Bourgogne to expand production. The Bourgogne and Chablis share bright lemony fruits supported by lively acidity (The Bourgogne is a blend of a third from Chablis with two thirds from Mâcon. It sells at around the same price as the Petit Chablis). Petit Chablis, Chablis, and premier crus Vaillons and Séchet are handled in stainless steel. Élevage is twelve months, a bit longer for grand crus. The house style of bright fruits with fresh acidity continues from Chablis to the Vaillons, coming out to full effect in a cooler year like 2016, and more rounded in a warmer year like 2015. In a typical year, these will be vins de garde that will benefit from a few years aging. "Séchet is the most mineral and tense of the left bank premier crus," Samuel says.

Mont de Milieu is more concentrated than Vaillons, but the full effect of the right bank shows with Montée de Tonnerre, where there is more weight to balance those bright fruits. Mont de Milieu and Montée de Tonnerre have partial aging in oak (20% in tonneaux), and the grand crus age in tonneaux (500 liters). Mont de Milieu may offer the most classic representation of Chablis. Montée de Tonnerre is very close to grand cru in quality. Bougros is a continuation from the right bank premier crus, with more subtle impressions of texture, Vaudésir is deeper, and Les Preuses shows its pedigree in great finesse. Some wood spice impressions show on the grand crus on release. There is a clear consistency of style from left bank premier crus to right bank premier crus to grand crus, with increasingly fine texture and more subtle flavor impressions. Obviously the proof will come in a few years time, but all the signs are that the premier and grand crus have great aging potential.

Domaine Billaud Simon ✶✶

◎ *1, Quai De Reugny, BP 46, 89800 Chablis*

☎ *(33) 03 86 42 10 33*

✉ *Catherine Lesueur*

@ *contact@billaud-simon.com*

🌐 *www.billaud-simon.com*

🍾 *Montée de Tonnerre*

🚫 ⚒

🍇 🕐 *17 ha; 150,000 bottles*

[map p. 21]

The domain originated in a marriage between Jean Billaud and Renée Simon before the second world war, bringing together the vineyards from two viticultural families, and their son Bernard Billaud ran the domain until it was sold to Faiveley in 2014. Samuel Billaud had been the winemaker until he left to form his own domain (he obtained some of the vineyards when the domain was sold in 2014). Faiveley effectively obtained two thirds of the vineyards and the winery. Behind the gracious old house where tastings are held is a large cuverie, constructed in 1991. Holdings are divided into about forty separate plots, with only six larger than a hectare, but more than half are in premier or grand crus.

In winemaking, there are two Billaud Simons. Going round the cuverie, there are lots of stainless steel tanks, and a rather small barrel room with a mix of barriques and demi-muids. The larger group of wines, about 80% of production, comprises Cuvées Haute Tradition; these are vinified exclusively in stainless steel, and range from Petit Chablis to grand crus. The smaller group of Cuvées Prestige has at least some oak maturation, 20% for Chablis Tête d'Or (which comes from a special plot just below Montée de Tonnerre), 10% for Fourchaume, 60% for Mont de Milieu, and 100% for Blanchots. Vaudésir was switched from stainless steel to 100% oak as an experiment in 2011, because it was always too closed previously. I have the feeling that Bernard's heart lies with the stainless steel cuvées, "All oak is old, new oak would be too marked," he says. Freshness is the quality that is most emphasized in tasting, and is marked in the Haute Tradition series, which shows traditional zesty character. It's unclear whether and how the style may change under Faiveley's ownership.

Jean-Marc Brocard   *

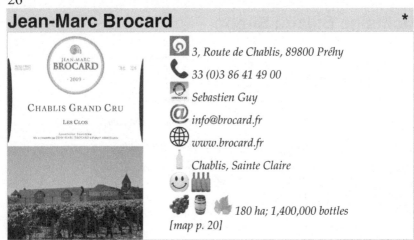

3, Route de Chablis, 89800 Préhy

33 (0)3 86 41 49 00

Sebastien Guy

info@brocard.fr

www.brocard.fr

Chablis, Sainte Claire

180 ha; 1,400,000 bottles
[map p. 20]

Jean-Marc created the domain in 1973 without any vineyards. The first vineyards were a couple of hectares inherited by his wife, just next to the fifteenth century church that is adjacent to the present winery. The domain occupies a rather splendid and vast modern building dating from 1984 in the middle of the vineyards just outside the village of Préhy. The building has a salle de vinification full of large foudres and some concrete eggs. Just below and partly out of sight is a more industrial-looking group of buildings (built in 2001) where the cuveries with stainless steel tanks are located. Jean-Marc has now retired and the domain is run by his son Julien and other members of the family. Today this is the largest family owned domain in Chablis.

Brocard is organic, but Julien is an enthusiast for biodynamics, and makes a separate range of wines under his own label from biodynamic vineyards. They are vinified and aged exclusively in old foudres; they include three cuvées from Chablis AOP, two grand cru, and Les Preuses. They are presented in a special bottle with a wax seal, and are just a little more expensive than the J. M. Brocard wines, which have a more extensive range with Petit Chablis, four cuvées of Chablis, five premier crus, and five grand crus. The J.M. Brocard range is extended by Bourgogne Blanc and Rouge, and local wines from the Auxerrois. Vinification varies for the J.M. Brocard wines, from stainless steel for Chablis, to a mixture of stainless steel and oak for premier crus, to all oak for grand crus. All the oak is old: "No new oak, that's not our style, it's just not for us," says Sébastien Guy, Julien's brother-in-law, who is charge of exports and mans the tasting room.

The Brocard house style tends to elegance, with fruits showing as light citrus against balanced acidity, never anything to excess. The same style runs through the whole range, with finesse on the palate, intensity increasing along the range, with more subtle flavor variety. The Julien Brocard wines follow the same stylistic imperatives, but tend to have more presence on the palate due to an extremely fine granular texture; perhaps this comes from the aging in foudres.

For both J.M. Brocard and Julien Brocard, the Vaudevey premier cru is just a tad deeper than the Chablis, and the real impression of premier crus comes with Montmains for J.M. Brocard, where the characteristic delicacy of the house style really shows, and Côte de Léchet for Julien Brocard. J.M. Brocard's Fourchaume, matured in foudres, is quite forceful for the house, but retains elegance. Comparing Les Preuses from J.M. Brocard with Julien Brocard is interesting because both are aged in foudres: both show the characteristic delicacy of this grand cru, but Julien's has more presence on the palate due to its exceptionally fine structure. Also matured in foudres, J.M. Brocard's Vaudésir has a little more weight, and Les Clos has the most presence on the palate of any of the crus, although showing its usual austerity.

La Chablisienne *

⊙ 8, Boulevard Pasteur, 89800 Chablis

📞 (33) 03 86 42 89 98

Ⓒ Le Cveau

@ caveau@chablisienne.fr

⊕ www.chablisienne.com

🍾 Fourchaume

😊 🍾🍾🍾

🟫🟫 🚜 1300 ha; 8,000,000 bottles

[map p. 21]

This important cooperative started in 1923 as a means for individual growers to sell their wines, blending and selling in bulk to negociants. In the 1950s, La Chablisienne made a transition to taking musts, and producing wine for direct sale. It has a splendid modern facility with a constant stream of visitors to its spacious tasting room. Representing 300 growers, today it accounts for around a quarter of all production in Chablis, including cuvées from 12 premier crus and 4 grand crus.

Vinification varies with the level of appellation: Petit Chablis and Chablis are vinified in steel, premier crus in 25% oak, and grand crus in 50% oak. There are three cuvées of Chablis: Finage comes from young vines, Sereine has some old vines, and Venerable comes from vines over 40 years old.

The cooperative actually purchased the estate of Château Grenouilles in 2003, which gave it ownership of most of the grand cru of Grenouilles. There are two cuvées: Fiefs de Grenouilles comes from young vines, and Château Grenouilles comes from the old vines, and is the top wine from La Chablisienne, even a little more powerful and aromatic than Les Clos. The differences between the various premier and grand crus stand out—in fact tasting the range offers an unusual opportunity because few producers have so many different crus—and there is good representation of vintage character. The wines are reliable with good typicity.

Domaine de Chantemerle   *

◎ *3, Place Des Côtats, 89800 La Chapelle-Vaupelteigne*

📞 *(33) 03 86 42 18 95*

👤 *Francis Boudin*

@ *dom.chantemerle@orange.fr*

🌐 *www.chablis-baudin.com*

🍾 *Fourchaume*

🚶 🍾🍾🍾

🍇 🚜 *16.5 ha; 25,000 bottles*

[map p. 20]

Domaine de Chantemerle has various names. It is also is known as Domaine Adhémar & Francis Boudin, or alternatively as Boudin Père & Fils. Adhémar Boudin was the son of a cooper, who created the domain the 1960s, but reacted to the family background by refusing to use any wood in his wines. His son, Francis, continues the tradition of avoiding all wood. "This is to avoid masking the aromas of Chardonnay or hardening or drying out the wine." All vinification is in cement. (The artisanal nature of the operation is indicated by a note of protest when I asked whether stainless steel was used.) Winemaking is natural, with whole bunch pressing followed by fermentation with indigenous yeasts.

The domain occupies a large square where most of the surrounding buildings seem to be part of the Boudin operation. Madame comes down from the family residence to open the tasting room, but tasting is a bit restricted as most of the wines have been sold out. Madame points to a few crates and says, "That's all that's left!" The range is smaller than most producers of similar size: Chablis (12 ha), Fourchaume (5 ha), and l'Homme Mort (a very small production from only 22 areas that is not exported). They are bottled under labels of either Boudin or Chantemerle, but the wine is the same. The style is clean and fruity, with citrus flavors predominating.

Jean Collet et Fils   *

📍 *15, Avenue De La Liberté , 89800 Chablis*

📞 *(33) 03 86 42 11 93*

👤 *Dominique Collet*

@ *collet.chablis@wanadoo.fr*

🌐 *www.domaine-collet.fr*

🍾 *La Forêt*

😊 🍾

🍇 🌿 *50 ha; 200,000 bottles*

[map p. 21]

The domain is housed in a modern facility on the outskirts of Chablis. Tastings take place in the large cave underneath. The domain was created by Jean Collet in 1952, although the family had already been in wine for a long time. The domain started with less than a hectare. Jean's son, Gilles, took over in 1989, and his son, Romain, started in 2009. Grapes come only from the estate, except for some Crémant. There are 2 ha of Petit Chablis, half of the vineyards are Chablis AOP (including a Vieilles Vignes), and the rest are premier and grand cru. Vaillons is the largest holding at 9 ha; "it is an assemblage of plots that truly reflects Vaillons," says Romain. Altogether there are 10 cuvées in Chablis.

Everything is fermented in stainless steel, but aging depends on the wine. Petit Chablis, Chablis, and some premier crus are handled only in stainless steel. Some premier crus are partly or wholly aged in oak, usually old (but with small proportions of new wood for some cuvées), using a range of sizes from barriques or demi-muids to large (3,000 liter) vats.

"You find our style in tension and minerality, according to the vintage," Romain says. "My father used to go for late maturity, but I harvest a bit sooner to keep acidity." The varying use of oak makes it difficult to define a single style. The Chablis conveys that sense of lively acidity and minerality, strengthened in Montmains, which is matured in stainless steel. Butteaux and La Forêt, which are within Montmains, are aged in wood: Butteaux has more tension and Forêt has greater richness. Vaillons has a classic balance between minerality and fruits. The right bank premier crus, Mont de Milieu and Montée de Tonnerre (aged in barriques), show as richer than the left bank premier crus. Although the grand crus, Valmur and Les Clos, see only a small amount of new oak, they show some spiciness. The unifying character is that sense of balancing the fruits against lively acidity.

Domaine Daniel Dampt et fils   *

1, chemin des Violettes Milly, 89800 Chablis

(33) 03 86 42 47 23

Daniel, Vincent, & Sébastien Dampt

domaine.dampt.defaix@wanadoo.fr

www.chablis-dampt.com

Beauroy

23 ha; 180,000 bottles

[map p. 20]

It is a bit tricky to keep track of all the Dampt domains. Domaine Daniel Dampt was formed when Daniel Dampt joined his vineyards with those of his father–in–law, Jean Defaix. Daniel has now been joined by his two sons, Vincent and Sébastien. The domain has 21 ha, including five premier crus, but because they do not own any grand crus, in 2008 they formed Maison Dampt to extend the range with a negociant activity. This allows the Dampts to add Bougros, Valmur, and Les Clos to the portfolio. In addition, Vincent and Sébastien each have 7 ha in their own name, including Chablis and some premier crus, which are vinified under the names of Domaine Vincent Dampt and Domaine Sébastien Dampt. "The aim of forming the family group and working all together was to bottle all our production," explains Vincent. All the wines are produced at the modern cellars in Milly, built in 1989 on the outskirts of the town. A new tasting room has been added next to the stockage facility, with splendid views across the vineyards over the town of Chablis to the grand crus.

Everything is vinified and matured in stainless steel, except for some oak used for the grand crus. "Stainless steel allows us to keep all the typicity of Chablis, with freshness and fruitiness, we like to make delicate wines without too much weight," Vincent says. Grand crus are vinified in old barriques. The barriques are at least three years old, but Vincent thinks even that would be too much for the premier crus. There is no battonage or racking. "The problem with battonage is that you can get richness but lose a lot of fruit, and we prefer to preserve the minerality in the wines. Sometimes using oak barrels hides the identity of the terroir," Vincent believes.

The Chablis is delicate, even a little aromatic, and then the impressions of minerality start with the premier crus. The left bank wines are more mineral than the right bank wines. Vaillons has a powerful expression of minerality. The Dampts have three different climats in Vaillons, and Les Lys is a special bottling from old vines—"it's probably the only north-facing vineyard in Chablis," says Vincent—which is a more concentrated and intense version of Vaillons. Côte de Léchet shows the most overt acidity of the premier crus, enhancing the sense of minerality, with salinity coming in at the end. "It always ages well, with increasing minerality," Vincent says. Beauroy is quite rounded, Fourchaume is in the same style but deeper. Les Clos is quite rich. Vincent recommends that the premier crus should be started about five years after the vintage.

Jean et Sébastien Dauvissat

*

3, Rue De Chichée, 89800 Chablis

(33) 03 86 42 14 62

Evelyne & Sébastien Dauvissat

jean.dauvissat@wanadoo.fr

www.chablisjsdauvissat.com

Vaillons

11 ha; 45,000 bottles

[map p. 21]

The name reflects the last two generations who have been charge of this domain, which has been in the family since 1899. It is one of several domains lining the street out of Chablis to Chichée, and you would never suspect that behind the front door lies a charming courtyard in front of the family house, which dates from the seventeenth century. Just to one side are stairs leading down to the caves underneath. Jean Dauvissat started bottling in the seventies, and slowly increased until all production was estate bottled. Since his death in an accident, the domain has been run by his wife Evelyne and son Sébastien. This is a small estate with three premier crus and one grand cru.

The wines have quite a full style. Montmains and Vaillons show stone and citrus fruits with an edge of minerality. In addition to the Vaillons *tout court*, there are two cuvées from *climats* within Vaillons. The Vieilles Vignes cuvée comes from 82-year-old vines in the Chatains *climat*. This is one of the two exceptions to the rule that the wines are vinified and aged in stainless steel "to keep freshness." Matured half in stainless steel and half in barriques—"but no new wood," Evelyne emphasizes—the wine is kept for two years before assemblage and bottling. Everything is intensified: it is simultaneously richer, rounder, and more mineral. The other *climat* in Vaillons is Séchet. "After the old vines, we will taste the Séchet, it is completely different," says Evelyne. This has more overt acidity, and a greater sense of salinity. Ever conscious of terroir, explaining the differences between the cuvées, Evelyne says that, "Montmains has clay, Vaillons is more calcareous, and Séchet is *really* calcareous." The grand cru, Les Preuses, is matured like the Vaillons Vieilles Vignes in cuve and barrique. Depending on the year, the wines tend to peak about five years after the vintage. The domain still offers older wines because is the policy is that, "We try to sell wines to our clients that are ready to drink."

Domaine Vincent Dauvissat

8, Rue Emile Zola, 89800 Chablis

(33) 03 86 42 11 58

Vincent Dauvissat

dauvissat.vincent@wanadoo.fr

La Forêt

🚫 ⚙

🍇 ⃝ 14 ha; 70,000 bottles

[map p. 21]

Dauvissat's approach was epitomized for me the first time I visited, when I asked Vincent how he decided on the length of élevage. Slightly startled at the naivety of the question, he shrugged, and said simply, "The wine tells me."

Without question, this is one of Chablis's top domains, making wines with rare intensity. Fermentation is mostly in cuve, but élevage is in old barriques (the average age of the barriques is ten years). "The fact that the wine matures in a container that breathes brings out the terroir for me," Vincent says, "but new oak loses the subtlety of terroir, the delicacy on the finish, I don't like that." Are there any differences in viticulture and vinification between the cuvées? "No, no, it's the same work in the vineyards and the cave. The only difference in élevage is the Petit Chablis, which has only 9 months, everything else is a year." So the differences are all due to terroir.

Half of the vineyards are in premier crus and a quarter in grand crus; average vine age is around 50 years. La Forêt and Vaillons are mineral, Preuses the most delicate, and Les Clos verges on austere until it develops that classic edge of anise. Is Les Clos always best? "Well each cru has its style. Clos is always the most powerful, but Preuses has its own distinct aromatic spectrum." Viticulture is biodynamic, but, "I'm a peasant, and need to be practical and efficient, so holding to the phases of the moon is tempered by the weather."

There is nothing less than exceptional here: on a visit in 2014, we were discussing the aging of Les Clos, when Vincent said, "Of course it ages well, but the Petit Chablis also ages, the 2012 will last twenty years." He proved his point by bringing out a 1996 Petit Chablis, which was mature but still lively. Some wines are bottled under the alternative label of Dauvissat-Camus.

Domaine Jean-Paul et Benoît Droin ✱✱

Chablis Premier Cru
Montée de Tonnerre
WHITE BURGUNDY WINE
APPELLATION CHABLIS PREMIER CRU CONTRÔLÉE
Mise en bouteilles à la Propriété par
Jean-Paul & Benoît DROIN
Propriétaires-Viticulteurs à Chablis · Yonne · France

🔘 *14 Bis, Rue Jean Jaurés, 89800 Chablis*

📞 *(33) 03 86 42 16 78*

📇 *Benoît Droin*

@ *benoit@jeanpaulbenoit-droin.fr*

🌐 *www.jeanpaul-droin.fr*

🍾 *Montée de Tonnerre*

🚫 ⚒

🍇 🗝 *26 ha; 185,000 bottles*
[map p. 21]

This family domain has been passed from father to son for fourteen genera-tions. Benoît has been in charge since the end of the 1990s. A new cuverie was built in 1999 on the road at the foot of the grand crus, but the elegant tast-ing room remains in the cave under the old family house in town. The domain has grown from 8 ha under Benoît's grandfather to its present size, with a range extending from Petit Chablis to nine premier and five grand crus. Only a few hectares are actually owned by the domain; most are owned by various members of the family, but worked by the domain.

Two generations ago the wines had no oak exposure, but oak was intro-duced in the 1980s, and the domain is now one of the leading producers of oaked premier and grand crus. Petit Chablis (from a single plot on Portlandian soil just above the grand crus) and Chablis (from several plots totaling 9 ha on the other side of the river) are produced in stainless steel. After fermentation in stainless steel, premier and grand crus are matured in a mix of cuves and oak barriques for about 10 months until assemblage just prior to bottling. Oak us-age for the crus at first was up to 100%, but "has been reduced from 15 years ago to bring out terroir and elegance," explains Benoit. Today the premier crus (9 ha total) see from 20-40% oak, and the grand crus (4 ha total) from 40-50%.

Accentuated by recent vintages, the style is on the fuller side for Chablis, sometimes quite Burgundian, more fruit-driven than savory, with Montée de Tonnerre usually beating out Montmains as the best premier cru, Grenouilles showing as the fullest grand cru, and Les Clos more austere. "The premier crus you can drink when very young, with the freshness for 2 or 3 years, after that wait until 7-10 years. It's a real pity when people say, I don't want to drink it young, I'll wait 3 years. That puts them right into the closed period, when they lose freshness but haven't gained complexity," Benoît says. In effect the mes-sage is, drink them young or drink them old.

Domaine Drouhin-Vaudon   *

 Chemin du Moulin-Chichée, 89800 Chablis, France

 (33) 03 80 24 68 88

 Denis Méry

@ maisondrouhin@drouhin.com

 www.drouhin-vaudon-chablis.com

 Montmains

38 ha; 200,000 bottles

[map p. 20]

The wines here used to be labeled as Joseph Drouhin—the Chablis AOP was described as Domaine de Vaudon Chablis, which caused some confusion—but since 2008 have been described as Drouhin-Vaudon to emphasize its separate identity. The domain takes its name from the old water mill, the Moulin de Vaudon, which was built in the eighteenth century. The Drouhins come from Chablis, and although most of their vineyards are now on the Côte d'Or, they have always had vineyards here. Hidden away at the entrance to the village, the property is located in an extensive park, and as an old water mill, the building straddles the river.

The vineyards in Chablis amount to almost half of the Drouhin's total vineyard holdings in Burgundy. They include seven premier crus and four grand crus. There is only a press room at the property, and the must is transferred immediately by tanker to Beaune, where vinification and aging take place. There are plans to build a winery in Chablis, but these were delayed when the Drouhins made a further acquisition in Oregon; they have become a far-flung company.

Wines come from both estate and purchased grapes; the balance varies widely, depending on the year. Wines made from estate grapes are labeled Propriétés de la Famille Drouhin. Chablis and premier crus are handled exclusively in stainless steel; grand crus are aged in demi-muids (600 liter). The style tends to freshness; indeed, Drouhin seems to have retained the typicity of Chablis better than many in its 2015s, with freshness dominating the palate, more tightly wound for the left bank, more obviously softened by some fat on the right bank. Perhaps the most classic representation of Chablis is the tightly wound Séchet premier cru; Montmains is a little rounder. On the right bank, Mont de Milieu is classic, with just a touch of that right bank fat, while Vaudésir is deeper and spicier, and Les Clos shows its austerity.

Domaine Nathalie et Gilles Fèvre *

Route de Chablis, 89800 Fontenay Près Chablis

(33) 03 86 18 94 47

Gilles Fèvre

fevregilles@wanadoo.fr

www.nathalieetgillesfevre.com

Fourchaume

50 ha; 120,000 bottles

[map p. 20]

"We are an old family of Chablis, related to William Fèvre. My branch of the family has always been in Fontenay, my grandfather founded the La Chablisienne coop, and my father was President for many years. Nathalie was cellarmaster at the coop for ten years. In 2003 we decided to form our own domain, so we left La Chablisienne. We had 12-13 ha, and we built a small winery. In 2003 our parents retired and gave us their vineyards, so now we have 50 ha, including a range of 15 appellations from Petit Chablis to grand cru. All our vines are around the village, basically between here and the grand crus," says Gilles Fèvre. The largest holdings are in premier cru Fourchaume and grand cru Les Preuses. The Fèvres have not entirely deserted the coop, as they sell about a third of their grapes to La Chablisienne. The wines are sometimes labeled as Marcel et Blanche Fèvre by way of tribute to Gilles' grandparents.

The style here tends to freshness, often with attractive herbal notes and a sense of fragrancy, running through the range. but intensifying from Petit Chablis, to Chablis, to premier cru, and to grand cru. Vinification focuses on stainless steel, but some wood is used for Valourent and Les Preuses. "We want to keep the freshness and minerality. We think 30% wood is enough," Nathalie says. "Chablis should be tense and mineral." As the premier crus come from the right bank, they tend to have that sense of greater roundness to soften the minerality, but Fourchaume retains the light, almost fragrant, impression that typifies the domain. Coming from a plot with more clay in Fourchaume, Valourent is richer, certainly the roundest of the cuvées, with a glycerinic sheen in warm years. That same sheen shows on grand cru Les Preuses. "Vaulorent is the cuvée with most character, it is perhaps less serious than Preuses, but it is the reference of the domain," Nathalie says. Gilles thinks the premier crus should be enjoyed at about 4-5 years; approaching ten years, they tend to show some tertiary development.

Domaine William Fèvre ★★

10, Rue Jules Rathier, 89800 Chablis

(33) 03 86 18 14 37

Alain Marcuello

caveau@williamfevre.com

www.williamfevre.fr

Valourent

78 ha; 500,000 bottles

[map p. 21]

The domain owes its present position to William Fèvre, the tenth generation in his family, who built it up to its present size from 7 ha after he took over in 1957. Half of the 90 individual parcels are in premier or grand crus. William was a significant figure in Chablis, trying to maintain quality, and arguing against the expansion of the seventies. With no one to succeed him, he sold to Champagne Henriot in 1998, and Didier Seguier came from Bouchard to run the domain.

A large winery at the edge of town has a splendid view of the slope of grand crus, and there's a spacious tasting room and bistro in the town center. The domain produces wines separately from estate and purchased grapes: estate wines state "Domain" discreetly on the label. Overall about half the grapes are purchased, but they go mostly into Petit Chablis and Chablis.

The style has changed significantly since the takeover: Fèvre used to show new oak, but now there is none. Didier vinifies Petit Chablis in cuve, and uses only 5-10% oak for Chablis. Premier and grand crus have around 40-60% oak, but "nothing gets more than 70% oak, and nothing spends more than six months in oak," he says. After six months in barriques, assemblage is followed by six months more in cuve.

The style continues to be on the ripe and powerful side for Chablis, and oak sometimes remains noticeable in young wines (although less so in recent vintages). The impressive range includes six grand crus and eight grand crus, but William would surely have cringed at the latest cuvée, "hipster" Chablis in a bottle that glows in the dark.

Domaine Garnier et Fils *

Chemin De Méré, 89144 Ligny-Le-Chatel

+33 03 86 47 42 12

Xavier & Jérôme Garnier

info@chablis-garnier.com

www.chablis-garnier.com

Montmains

24 ha; 200,000 bottles

[map p. 20]

"We are very happy with out short history, it has allowed us to show our own style," says winemaker Jérôme Garnier, who established the domain together with his brother Xavier, who manages the vineyards. "We are not like other growers, we make round and fat wines, from grapes with good maturity, we are not in the acidic line." Located in the northernmost village of the Chablis appellation, the domain has vineyards of Petit Chablis and Chablis located on Portlandian soil. "It's less chalky and we have more clay, we want to express the fruit in the wine."

"Our father was a farmer, and I and my brother decided to plant vineyards. We also buy grapes from premier crus and grand crus to complement the range, as well as some red grapes. We try to give the same expression to the wine from the grapes we buy, generally our style is rich with a powerful body. Most growers want to start harvest earlier because they want to keep freshness, but we want exactly the opposite—ripe and rich." The first vintage was 1999.

Petit Chablis comes from Lignorelles and ages 6 months in stainless steel. It's quite full on the palate, and nutty in the background. Chablis is the major part of production; a blend from all the estate plots, it ages 10-12 months in stainless steel. It's fuller on the palate, with a glossy sheen, more inclined to stone fruits than citrus. Grains Dorées comes from specific estate plots, with two years aging, starting with 60% in wood and 40% in cuve, and is round, rich, and soft. "I think when this cuvée is bottled, it's at maturity," Jérôme says.

Premier and Grand Crus age for 16-18 months in a mix of demi-muids and foudres, with no new oak except when it's necessary to replace a barrel. "All the oak comes from Austria because it doesn't give a wood impression to the wine." Mont de Milieu has a sense of reserve, Côte de Jouan moves farther in a spicy direction, Montmains is full and soft with a spicy texture, and a sense of density moving towards grand cru, while Fourchaumes is something of a break with the style, moving more towards the traditional freshness of Chablis. Grand Crus Vaudésir ages for two years in demi-muids, and has a textured, spicy impression, dense but not immediately so opulent as Montmains because of greater structure. In some years there is also a cuvée from Les Clos.

Domaine Guilhem & Jean-Hugues Goisot *

30, Rue Bienvenu Martin, 89530 Saint-Bris-Le-Vineux

(33) 03 86 53 35 15

Guilhem Goisot

domaine.jhg@goisot.com

www.goisot.com

Sauvignon St. Bris, Exogyra virgula

30 ha; 160,000 bottles

This family domain, whose name refers to father and son, occupies a pretty winery building in the center of St. Bris. "We've been in the village since the fifteenth or sixteenth century; members of the family have been innkeepers or tonneliers, but there's always been at least one vigneron each generation," says Guilhem Goisot. "I'm the seventh direct generation to run this domain. My great grandfather planted most of it." The domain includes Bourgogne Aligoté, Irancy, Bourgogne Côtes d'Auxerrois, and Sauvignon de St. Bris. The cuvées represent different soils or altitudes: most of the terroirs are Kimmeridgian, with varying extents of clay, but exposures and altitudes vary. Pinot Noir or Chardonnay are planted on south-facing sites, Sauvignon Blanc is planted elsewhere. There are three different cuvées from St. Bris and five from the Côtes d'Auxerrois. "All the names of the cuvées represent places—we don't use people's names etc." The names are a better indication of sources than the appellation, as Coys de Garde (for example) is Côtes d'Auxerre for Pinot Noir or Chardonnay, but St. Bris for Sauvignon. Vinification is the same for all wines, and the fascinating thing is that the same style of rounded citrus fruits supported by crisp acidity, some more mineral than others, transcends cépage and runs through the Auxerrois and the St. Bris. This makes for a very Burgundian take on the Sauvignon Blanc variety, and as a result, I find the St. Bris cuvées to be the most interesting.

Domaine Jean-Pierre et Corinne Grossot   *

4, Route Mont De Milieu, 89800 Fleys

(33) 03 86 42 44 64

Corinne & Jean-Pierre Grossot

info@chablis-grossot.com

www.chablis-grossot.com

Vaucoupin

18 ha; 80,000 bottles
[map p. 20]

Located in the village of Fleys a little to the east of the town of Chablis, the domain was created by Jean-Pierre Grossot in 1980; previously his parents and grandparents sold grapes to the coop. Today Jean-Pierre works with his daughter Eve, who is taking over winemaking. The vineyards were converted to organic in 2012 (previously viticulture had been lutte raisonnée); in fact, Jean-Pierre was in the vineyards with an organic inspector when I arrived. Organic viticulture was interrupted by bad conditions in 2016 but then resumed. The major part of the vineyards (13 ha) is in appellation Chablis, giving a cuvée that is about half of all production. A small (1.5 ha) parcel just near the domain, with extremely calcareous soil, is the basis for a separate cuvée, La Part des Anges. There are five premier crus, occupying 5 ha altogether. Almost everything is vinified and then matured on the lees in stainless steel, but Mont de Milieu and Les Fourneaux see a quarter to a third élevage in old oak. The cellar has a mix of tonneaux and barriques. After six months there is assemblage, and then a further eight months in cuve. The style offers fairly direct fruits for the Chablis and the La Part des Anges cuvée, a sense of more complexity with the little-known premier cru Côte de Troemes, and then savory, herbal impressions strengthen going up the hierarchy to Vaucoupin and Fourchaume. At the premier cru level, house style is typified by a fine impression with precision of fruits. Wines are made for enjoyment in the years immediately after release.

Domaine Laroche **

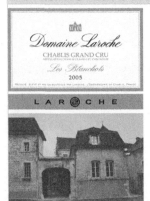

L'Obediencerie, 22 rue Louis Bro, 89800, Chablis

(33) 03 86 42 89 00

Thierry Bellicaud

info@larochewines.com

www.larochewines.com

Montmains

90 ha; 5,000,000 bottles [map p. 21]

One of the largest producers in Chablis, Domaine Laroche has expanded enormously since Michel Laroche made his first crop from 6 ha in 1967. There is a tasting room in the center of Chablis, and the winery is nearby, behind an old monastery dating from the ninth century. Today the estate includes 62 ha of Chablis AOP and another 21 ha of premier crus, making it one of the larger producers in Chablis.

The Chablis St. Martin cuvée under Domaine Laroche comes from the best lots of estate vineyards (roughly 70% of total); the other 30% is blended with purchased grapes and is the simple Chablis cuvée, just labeled Laroche. You have to look carefully at the label to see a difference. Chablis is vinified exclusively in stainless steel; oak is used for premier and grand crus, varying from 15-25% for the premier crus, and around 30% for grand crus.

The style tends to be relatively fruity, but of course varies with the cru. "Beauroy is south facing and warmer, Vaudevey on the other side of the hill is more north facing. Like a red wine, the south exposure favors phenolic development; Beauroy is rounder than Vaudevey, which is straighter and more mineral. We do the same work in the vines but the wines are completely different. Vaillons is another warm spot, if we let the vines ripen as much as they would like, you would lose the terroir," says vineyard manager Gilles Madelin. In grand crus, as the largest proprietor of Blanchots, Laroche makes a special cuvée, La Réserve de l'Obédience, based on selecting the best lots by blind tasting: here oak has varied from 30% to 100% over the past few years.

Laroche is a modernist not only in style, but in moving to screwcaps. "Michel Laroche was dark red when he saw cork manufacturers because he was fed up with quality," explains Sandrine Audegond at the domain. From 2006, premier and grand crus were available with either screwcap or cork, so the buyer could choose, but in 2016 there was a move back to cork. Laroche expanded beyond Chablis, first in southern France and then in Chile and South Africa, before merging with JeanJean to form the Advini wine group in 2010. Laroche also owns Mas La Chevalière in Languedoc.

Domaine Long-Depaquit *

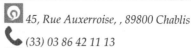

45, Rue Auxerroise, , 89800 Chablis

(33) 03 86 42 11 13

Matthieu Mangenot

chateau-long-depaquit@albert-bichot.com

www.albert-bichot.com

Vaillons

65 ha; 420,000 bottles
[map p. 21]

"The styles are really different here. The common features of Chablis are freshness and minerality, but Bichot's style is to produce wine with fruity character. We work on the picking date, we don't want to lose the acidity, but we want the wine to show fruit, it needs to speak quickly," says winemaker Matthieu Mangenot. Founded at the time of the French Revolution, Long-Depaquit was purchased by Beaune negociant Albert Bichot in 1968; Bichot built it up from 10 ha to its present position as one of the major estates in Chablis. The splendid château dates from the eighteenth century; a new winery was constructed in 1991 and is presently being renovated and extended.

The Chablis is split into two parts: the best selection goes to Long Depaquit Chablis, the rest is labeled as Bichot. Everything is vinified in small tanks of stainless steel; the Chablis and some premier crus remain in cuve. Since the 1990s, the more important premier crus have seen 10-25% oak, and grand crus range from 25% to 100%; oak exposure lasts 6-8 months, after which assemblage is followed by another 9-12 months in cuve. The style is distinctly fruity, and you have to go halfway through the premier cru range really to see minerality. No extremes might be the motto of the house. The house style does have a lovely, smooth, silky balance, with extremely judicious use of oak. Grand crus show their terroir, especially Les Clos and the flagship La Moutonne, a monopole that is essentially part of Vaudésir. The style is similar at the much smaller Château de Viviers, which is also owned by Bichot.

Domaine des Malandes

11 route d'Auxerre, 89800 Chablis

(33) 03 86 42 41 37

Amandine Marchive

contact@domainedesmalandes.com

www.domainedesmalandes.com

Chablis, Tour du Roy

28 ha; 180,000 bottles
[map p. 21]

"The domain in Chablis was founded in 1972, but before that my father and grandfather were in La Chapelle—all my ancestors are in the cemetery there—they were farmers because it was impossible to make a living from the vineyard. So it is not exactly true if I tell you I come from a very old family of winemakers," says Lyne Marchive. "If global warming continues we may have to go back to growing crops and keeping animals. I've been the manager here for forty years and I will retire in December. I am leaving for the north of France, and my son (who has his own domain in Beaujolais), will take over winemaking. My daughter will take over sales."

The building is a rather commercial-looking warehouse just off the main road into Chablis (extended in 2014). The tasting is down in the cave, and has the one decorative feature of the building, a mural representing the vineyards of Chablis. There is a fair-sized range here, as there are plots all over the appellation, including five premier crus and two grand crus. Screwcaps are used for the Petit Chablis and Chablis. Petit Chablis and Chablis are produced only in steel, but the general procedure is to vinify partially (for the premier crus) or wholly (for the grand crus) in oak, and then to age only in steel. What is the advantage? "It's difficult to vinify in oak, it's much easier in tank. But when you vinify in oak, it's completely different, there is exchange, because of the bubbles released during fermentation, between wine and the oak. But after vinification, the oak has done its work in Chablis. To conserve the delicacy and freshness it's best to age in tank, you can lose it by aging in oak," Lyne explains.

The style is elegant and delicate, almost perfumed, and you really see the difference between the left bank, where minerality and salinity are more obvious, and the right bank, which is more rounded; but the balance is always subtle. The sense of fragrancy increases from Petit Chablis to Chablis, with a big step up to the Chablis Tour du Ray, which comes from a single vineyard of 62-year-old vines. The minerality with faint overtones of herbs and salinity of both Vaudevey and Montmains is true to Chablis's tradition. Moving to the right bank, "Fourchaume always has a more seductive style. You can find

Fourchaume that is richer than ours, but we are always the first to harvest because I want to showcase elegance." It is quite delicate for Fourchaume, with that understated sense of minerality typifying the house style. In the grand crus, Vaudésir (from a plot on the side of the shadow) is more feminine, while Les Clos (from a full south-facing plot) is typically is more masculine, with more sense of austerity. You can see where Lyne's heart is from a comment about vintages. "The 2016 vintage for me is purely Chablis. It is not very charming, but it is really for the people who love Chablis. 2015 is very charming."

La Manufacture ⃰

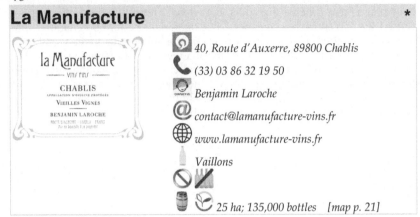

la Manufacture
—— vins fins ——
CHABLIS
APPELLATION D'ORIGINE PROTÉGÉE
VIEILLES VIGNES
BENJAMIN LAROCHE

🔘 40, Route d'Auxerre, 89800 Chablis

📞 (33) 03 86 32 19 50

👤 Benjamin Laroche

@ contact@lamanufacture-vins.fr

🌐 www.lamanufacture-vins.fr

🍾 Vaillons

🛢 🌱 25 ha; 135,000 bottles   [map p. 21]

Founded in 2012, this negociant is a project of Benjamin Laroche, a nephew of Michel Laroche (see profile). Benjamin spent ten years working at Laroche before starting his own enterprise. The name is a play on the origins of the word "manufacture," meaning made by hand. "We have a new model of micro-trading," says Benjamin's partner, Vanessa Gicquel. Basically the growers make the wine to Benjamin's specifications, then it is aged at La Manufacture's facility, which is effectively an aging cellar.

"We have a dozen producers who make wine for us, we have our own vats there, etc," Virginia explains. "We can have more variety of sources this way, but we maintain a style. Some of the producers make wine for themselves also, some mostly sell grapes or wine to the negociants or cooperative. Our winemakers are young, they know how to make a great wine from certain plots, if they sell it to others it's lost because it's blended out. Benjamin had to explain that we would value their work more, although it will be less productive."

Chablis and premier crus ferment in stainless steel, and grand crus ferment in barriques. Aging follows a traditional model in which more oak is used going up the hierarchy. "We use a lot of demi-muids, 1-2-year old but not new, because they don't hide the wine," Virginia says. Typically Chablis sees 25% demi-muids, premier cru Beauroy uses 30%, premier cru Vaillons uses 100%.

There are 16 cuvées in Chablis, including Petit Chablis, Chablis, premier crus, and six of the seven grand crus. Each cuvée comes from a single grower. The style tends towards fruity, tinged with minerality, intensifying from Petit Chablis to Chablis, and becoming more forceful with Beauroy. "This is always the most exuberant of our crus," Virginia says. The Vaillons Vieilles Vignes (from 45-year-old vines) makes a more subtle impression, with the fruits more subdued by the sense of minerality. Grand Cru Blanchots is smooth and weightier, with hints of spice. For me, Vaillons gives the most intense sense of the typicity of Chablis.

Other wines include red and white Bourgogne, and a Sauvignon St. Bris, which is quite exuberant. The Atelier range consists of red wines from the Côte d'Or, produced on a conventional negociant model.

Domaine Louis Michel ***

9, Boulevard De Ferrières, 89800 Chablis

(33) 03 86 42 88 55

Guillaume Michel

contact@louismicheletfils.com

www.louismicheletfils.com

Montée de Tonnerre

25 ha; 150,000 bottles

[map p. 21]

"Our policy is simply to make wines that represent the terroir of Chablis: fresh, pure and mineral," says Guillaume Michel. This translates to élevage in stainless steel. There has been no oak since 1969, and Louis Michel is now the pre-eminent domain for the unoaked style of Chablis. "My grandfather didn't like the taste of oak, and he didn't have a lot of time to maintain barrels in the cellar," Guillaume explains.

The domain stretches out along a street running down to the river. The old barrel cellars below have been renovated into a chic tasting room. The major difference between cuvées is the length of time in cuve before bottling: 6 months for Petit Chablis and Chablis, on average 12 months for premier crus, and 18 months for grand crus. While lees-aging in steel is common in Chablis, few others achieve the complexity of Louis Michel. Slow fermentation leads to rich extraction. After that, "premier and grand crus wines may be matured on lees but it's not systematic as we want to focus on purity and precision and avoid wines that would be too heavy. It would depend on the vintage. As far as Petit and Chablis is concerned, we do not mature on lees."

The balance of fruity to savory notes changes with each premier cru, but all share a delicious textured background, which often leads to confusion with oak aging. The emphasis is on bringing out terroir. "We have vineyards in all three parts of Montmains (including *climats* Butteaux and Forêt); my grandfather used to blend but I prefer to make separate cuvées. Montmains has more clay, Forêt has more limestone, Butteaux has more clay with larger lumps of Kimmeridgian limestone. Clay brings flesh and roundness, limestone brings minerality. Butteaux is an interesting intermediate. There are only a few 100 meters between the vineyards."

In the grand crus, Vaudésir is rich and savory. "There are two sides to Vaudésir. We are on the back, not the side that faces south. So this is not our ripest grand cru, but it is the only one of the grand crus that is expressive when young." Grenouilles is even fuller bodied, and Les Clos shows its usual austerity. These are wines that often can be drunk early, but this misses the complexity that develops later, after say 6 years for premier crus and 10 years for grand crus. Guillaume has a view: "I would say a premier cru needs at least 4-5 years, and depending on the vintage can last for 20 years. When you bottle the wine, for the first few months you can drink it, but then depending on the vintage it closes down."

Domaine Christian Moreau Père et Fils **

26, Avenue d'Oberwesel, 89800 Chablis

(33) 03 86 42 86 34

Fabien Moreau

contact@domainechristianmoreau.com

www.domainechristianmoreau.com

Vaillons, Cuvée Guy Moreau

11.5 ha; 135,000 bottles

[map p. 21]

This is nominally a new domain, but Christian Moreau is the sixth generation of winemakers in his family. Christian had been at the family estate of J. Moreau for thirty years when the company was sold to Boisset, but he kept the family vineyards, although grapes continued to be supplied to J. Moreau under contract until 2002, when the new domain started. The domain is housed in a utilitarian warehouse just across the bridge from the town center. "Our goal was to produce top quality Chablis," says Fabien Moreau, who has been involved in the domain with his father since the beginning. "The domain is basically me and my father, with a small vineyard crew. I'm the only person in the cellar."

Some grapes are purchased to increase volume for the Chablis, but the premier and grand crus come only from estate vineyards. "I don't like to say there's a Christian Moreau style, I want to respect each terroir," is how Fabien describes stylistic objectives. Oak is used for premier and grand crus, varying from 30-50% depending on the cru and the vintage. The Chablis and the Vaillons focus directly on fruit, but the Guy Moreau cuvée from a plot of old vines in Vaillons begins the move towards a more structured character, which accentuates through the grand crus. The flagship wine is Clos des Hospices, from a plot in Les Clos, which the Moreau family bought in 1904 from the Hospices; this has always been a big wine for Chablis.

Domaine Louis Moreau

*

DOMAINE
LOUIS MOREAU

CHABLIS 1ᴱᴿ CRU
VAULIGNOT
Appellation Chablis 1ᵉʳ Cru Contrôlée

📍 *10, Grande Rue, 89800 Beine*

📞 *(33) 03 86 42 87 20*

👤 *Frédérique Chamoy*

@ *contact@louismoreau.com*

🌐 *www.louismoreau.com*

🍾 *Vaillons*

😊 🍷

🍇 ☙ *45 ha; 250,000 bottles   [map p. 20]*

The Moreaus are an old family in Chablis, going back to 1814. Louis is the six generation. He holds three domains, two inherited and one that he established. Domaine de Biéville, created in 1965 by Louis's father, Jean-Jacques, produces Chablis AOP from a single holding of 45 ha (very rare in the area). Jean-Jacques also established Domaine du Cèdre Doré, another 5 ha, also producing Chablis AOP. Louis worked in California for ten years, and when he returned in 1992, he wanted to make his own wine. He created his own domain, which includes half of the vineyards that used to be leased to the family firm, J. Moreau (created by Jean-Jacques in the 1970s, but no longer in the family). Domaine Louis Moreau extends from Chablis AOP to grand crus, and represents just under a third of the production from all three domains. Wine is made at the domain headquarters, right on the road through Beine. Behind the ordinary front, there is a large warehouse-like facility for winemaking. A huge new facility for stockage has been built just round the corner, and next to it is a dedicated tasting room.

The attitude to winemaking is summarized by an offhand comment: "People are coming back, they are looking for real Chablis, without any oak." From Petit Chablis to grand cru, vinification is the same, in steel; then the wine is left on the fine lees. Blanchots and Valmur are exceptions that age in barrique. Petit Chablis and Chablis spend 4-5 months aging, premier crus take 8-10 months, and grand crus spend 12-18 months. Up to premier cru, bottling is Diam (agglomerated cork) or screwcap, depending on market, but grand crus stay under cork.

Louis Moreau says that, "The wines are upright and linear with good tension," which is a fair description. There is always a sense of minerality, often with a delicious saline catch on the finish. Chablis AOP and premier crus are textbook examples of the unoaked style. Les Clos tends to austerity, and Valmur has greater breadth, enhanced by its vinification and aging in oak.

Domaine Pattes Loup ★

⊚ *2, Grande-Rue Nicolas Droin 89800, Courgis*

📞 *(33) 03 86 41 46 38*

▢ *Thomas Pico*

@ *thomas.pico@pattes-loup.com*

⊕ *www.pattes-loup.com*

🍾 *Chablis, Vente d'Ange*

☺ 🍾

🍇 🏭 *25 ha*

[map p. 20]

Domaine de Bois d'Yver was the family domain, where Georges Pico planted most of the vines, but Thomas Pico wanted to work organically, so separated to found his own domain, which he called Pattes Loup. He started with 2.5 ha that his father gave him in 2007, and now makes wine from 25 ha, including Chablis and four premier crus. Georges Pico has now retired, but Thomas still makes wines for Domaine de Bois d'Yver from 10 ha. The domains are located in a building right at the end of the village, which was renovated in 2014. Operating on three levels, everything is gravity-fed.

Vinification takes place in stainless steel tanks and in concrete eggs. Chablis ages mostly in cuve, and the premier crus age in old oak. There are lots of very old barriques and some demi-muids (600 liter). Wines tasted from cuve have a forceful style that owes something to long élevage; in 2017 I tasted 2015s (including Chablis AOP) that will not be bottled until next year. The premier crus have will 30 months élevage this year, although usually it's 18 months. The wine calms down and becomes more integrated once in bottle, but still has a very lively style of lemony citrus flavors supported by bright acidity.

Usually the domain confines itself to Chablis, but low production forced a change. "Last year because of hail I bought some grapes and made a Vin de France Chardonnay," Thomas explains. The attitude here is committed artisanal. During the tasting, my companion remarked, "Now wine is more scientific." "No it isn't," Thomas shot back.

Domaine Gilbert Picq et Fils *

3, Route De Chablis, 89800 Chichée

(33) 03 86 42 18 30

Didier Picq

domaine.picq-gilbert@wanadoo.fr

Chablis, Vieilles Vignes

14 ha; 90,000 bottles
[map p. 20]

This tiny property is right in the center of Chichée, occupying a cluster of buildings on either side of the main road. The tasting room is in a very old but charming cave underneath. This is very much a family domain focused on the neighborhood: Didier Picq is the sixth generation, and works with his brother. "The Picqs have always produced their own wine," Didier says. A little reticent at first, Didier opens up with enthusiasm to describe the wines. Vinification is the same for all the wines: all in stainless steel, no wood. Only estate grapes are used. "If Vincent Dauvissat wanted to sell me grapes, I'd buy, but I haven't found any source I like."

There are two left bank premier crus, but four different cuvées from Chablis AOP, which represents more than half the domain. The style tends to be nicely rounded with herbal impressions on the palate. La Vaudécorse is a 1 ha single vineyard parcel, presenting more subtle herbal notes and finer texture than the Chablis *tout court*. The domain is well known for its Vieilles Vignes, which comes from 60-70-year old vines and has that extra density of old vines, together with a kick of richness at the end. Dessus La Carrière is a very stony 2 ha parcel giving wines with increased intensity. Premier cru Vaucoupin has a more mineral impression than the Chablis cuvées, with great purity of fruits. It shows the same style as the Chablis, but with greater subtlety of expression and more flavor variety on the palate. Vosgros makes a restrained mineral impression, not quite austere, but with great potential for aging.

Most of the production is exported, with the U.S. as the major market, focused on New York. In France you are more likely to find the wines in a restaurant than in a shop.

Domaine Pinson Frères *

 5, Quai Voltaire, 89800 Chablis

📞 (33) 03 86 42 10 26

Laurent Pinson

@ contact@domaine-pinson.com

🌐 www.domaine-pinson.com

Mont de Milieu

14 ha; 75,000 bottles
[map p. 21]

The Pinsons have been making wine in Chablis since the seventeenth century, but the domain was really created in its present form by Louis Pinson in the 1940s when he focused on producing and bottling his own Chablis. The name changed after his grandsons Laurent and Christophe came into the domain in the early 1980s and increased its size from an initial 4 ha. About half the vineyards are premier cru, and another quarter are in the grand cru Les Clos. Located at the edge of town on the Serein river, a new cuverie was built in 2004 with stainless steel fermentation cuves.

The domain is one of the arch exponents of the oaked style: after fermentation wines are transferred to barriques, using nine months élevage in 1- to 3-year-oak for premier crus, and a year for Les Clos, which includes 10% new oak. There's a special cuvée from Les Clos, Authentique, from older vines, which spends the first 6 months in entirely new oak, followed by 18 months in older oak. The same style at Pinson runs through the Chablis, premier crus, and grand crus. There's a faint note of apples on top of a tendency towards the savory, giving almost a piquant impression. Minerality is in the background. Pinson's premier and grand crus tend to be delicious when released, then after two or three years they close up: do not panic, but it's better not to touch them for the best part of a decade, until they open out again into a full, creamy style that brings a more subtle representation of the oak regime.

Patrick Piuze *

VENDANGES 2009

CHABLIS PREMIER CRU
LES FORÊTS

Patrick Piuze

25 rue Emile Zola, 89800 Chablis

33 (0)3 86 18 85 73

Patrick Piuze

p.piuze@patrickpiuze.com

www.patrickpiuze.com

Montée de Tonnerre

0 ha; 150,000 bottles
[map p. 21]

As a micro-negociant, Patrick Piuze makes an unusually wide range of cuvées. His winery in the heart of Chablis is an old building bought from Vocoret, larger than it appears at first, as it's connected by a tunnel under the road to caves on the other side. "This was constructed in the period when a Vocoret was the mayor of Chablis, it probably wouldn't be possible today," Patrick explains. What is the driving force to be a negociant in Chablis? "I wasn't born here, I came from Montreal. The only way to express a lot of terroirs is to be a negociant. We try to buy grapes we like from special sites, before we worry about having a specific appellation."

Production is 65% Petit Chablis or Chablis; 35% is premier and grand cru. Patrick harvests with his own team. "Choosing harvest date is one of the most important things. We are an early picker. A wine can have only one backbone. 90% of white wines in the world have an alcohol backbone, but we have an acid backbone. Our wines are never more than 12.3%." Petit Chablis is matured in cuve, Chablis in a mixture of cuve and barriques, and premier and grand crus are entirely in barrique. The style gets to full ripeness without excess, with a silky sheen to the fruits, a sense of stone fruits adding to the citrus and minerality of Chablis; yet always with that wonderfully moderate alcohol. A sense of tension counterpoised against elegant fruits runs through the range from premier crus to the more overtly full grand crus.

L & C Poitout *

📍 *3 Rue Laffitte, 89800 Chablis*

📞 *(33) 09 79 61 62 16*

 *Catherine Poitout*

@ *contact@lc-poitout.fr*

🌐 *lc-poitout.fr*

🍾 *Chablis, Les Venérés*

🍾 *Vin de France, l'Inextinct*

🍇 ⚲ *18.5 ha; 25,000 bottles*
[map p. 21]

Both from families involved with winemaking in Chablis, Catherine and Louis Poitout formed their own domain in 2011. "We started with many small parcels," explains Louis, "but they weren't all the true taste of Chablis, so we sold many in 2012 and bought others." Vinification is not fully organic, but no insecticides are used in the vineyards, which are ploughed using a horse. The domain is located in a charming old house on the banks of the Serein, with a modern tasting room.

The Petit Chablis comes from a plot overlooking Valmur, the Chablis Bienommé comes from the north, and keeps freshness, while Chablis Les Vénérées comes from old vines planted in 1946 and 1960. There are two premier crus: Les Fourneaux faces pure south, and Vaucoupin faces west. "The difference is enormous," says Louis.

So what is the true taste of Chablis? "The true taste of Chablis is mineral with the most simple vinification. We do exactly the same vinification for all cuvées. There is never any wood. Everything is kept as simple as possible," Louis explains. The Petit Chablis is a textbook example: simple, direct, and fruity. Chablis Bienommé is more restrained with the first impression of minerality; then Les Vénérées moves in a herbal direction, with a real sense of texture to the palate that makes you think of wood, "but there is none." Vaucoupin really brings out minerality, and Les Fourneaux is fuller and richer. "It's hot and in full sun, you lose minerality but gain roundness."

The most unusual wine comes from a tiny plot of 55 ares of old, ungrafted vines in the area of Petit Chablis. "In 2012 we were looking for parcels, and we found one that was in very bad condition. The vines had been cut at the base and everyone thought they would die, because they'd been cut at the graft, but they grew," Louis recalls. They turned out to be ungrafted. "The wine is labeled as Vin de France because it doesn't fit our idea of Petit Chablis," Louis says. Called L'Inextinct to reflect its origins, it shows great purity of fruits, richness on the palate, yet retains the lively acidity of Chablis. It's a rare experience.

Domaine Denis Race *

Rue Benjamin Constant, 89800 Chablis

(33) 03 86 42 45 87

Denis Race

domaine@chablisrace.com

www.chablisrace.com

Mont de Milieu

18 ha; 90,000 bottles

[map p. 21]

The entrance looks like a quiet shop front in a residential street, but underneath is a large cave that has been completely modernized. There's a dedicated tasting room at the front of the cave, and it's a mark of the hands-on nature of the operation that when visitors descend to the tasting room, the lady running the bottling line in the next room stops bottling and comes to manage a tasting. The estate was founded in the 1930s; Denis Race is the grandson of the founder, joined by his daughters Clare in 2005 (now the winemaker) and Marine in 2015.

The domain has moved to mechanical harvesting—Denis has not quite retired and still drives the tractor—then the grapes are pressed immediately in pneumatic presses. The domain is committed to stainless steel, and wines mature in cuve for 9-10 months before bottling and release. "It's true that wood adds something to the wine, but it's not what we are looking for. What we are after is something more natural," Clare says. Marine is a fan of barrels, so there's an experiment with wood in the form of three barriques, but this remains confined to a vey small cuvée.

There are three premier crus, of which Montmains is the most important with a total of 5 ha in several different parcels. One plot of 60-year-old vines is bottled separately as the Vieilles Vignes; the others are blended into the Montmains cuvée. The Chablis is relatively soft and a little aromatic, Montmains is broader and more restrained, Vaillons is more linear and more delicate, tilting in the direction of minerality, and Mont de Milieu broadens the herbal impressions with a typical touch of fat from the right bank. The Vieilles Vignes shows a real increase in concentration from the Montmains *tout court*.

Domaine François Raveneau   ★★★★

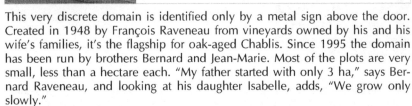

 *9, Rue de Chichée, BP 13, 89800 Chablis*

📞 *(33) 03 86 42 17 46*

Bernard Raveneau

📠 *(33) 03 86 42 45 55*

🍾 *Chapelot*

🚫 🍷

🍇 ⏱ *10 ha; 45,000 bottles*
[map p. 21]

This very discrete domain is identified only by a metal sign above the door. Created in 1948 by François Raveneau from vineyards owned by his and his wife's families, it's the flagship for oak-aged Chablis. Since 1995 the domain has been run by brothers Bernard and Jean-Marie. Most of the plots are very small, less than a hectare each. "My father started with only 3 ha," says Bernard Raveneau, and looking at his daughter Isabelle, adds, "We grow only slowly."

Élevage is the same for everything from Chablis to grand cru, with fermentation followed by aging for a year in old oak. A horizontal tasting at Raveneau is an education in the terroirs of Chablis. Consistency of style shows all the way from Chablis AOP (produced since 2007) to the grand cru Les Clos: fruits give an impression of being more textured than simply dense, with a savory overlay that turns in the direction of anise with time.

The Chablis is the most openly fruity; it is very good but the special character of Raveneau really starts with the premier crus. La Fôret (part of Montmains) isn't so much more intense as just shifting the balance a bit from fruity to savory, Butteaux (another part of Montmains) adds more mineral notes as do the Montmains and Vaillons. Chapelot (part of Montée de Tonnerre) is usually more steely and less powerful than the Montée de Tonnerre cuvée, which shows intimations of the power of the grand crus. Montée de Tonnerre is the largest cuvée, about a third of all production. Among the grand crus, Blanchots is usually broad, Valmur is more precise, Clos is always the most austere and backward.

What's the secret, I asked, what gives Raveneau Chablis its unique quality? "It's the origin, *travail attentif* in the vines. A chef would say that if the ingredients are top quality, there is no need for artifice: it's exactly the same with wine. There is no secret (except that) we never go to extremes here. Many people today say they do something special, such as biodynamics."

The steely minerality of the young wines begins to open out after about 5-6 years for premier crus and 8-10 years for grand crus. (Don't even think of opening Les Clos until it is close to 10 years old: it would be sheer vinicide.) Raveneau Chablis is virtually unique; unfortunately this is now also true of the price.

Domaine Servin

 20, Avenue d'Oberwesel, 89800 Chablis

(33) 03 86 18 90 00

François Servin

contact@servin.fr

www.servin.fr

Vaillons

36 ha; 250,000 bottles
[map p. 21]

The Servin family have owned vines in Chablis since the seventeenth century. Located in old buildings just across the river from the town center, the domain is run today by the seventh generation, François Servin, together with his brother-in-law. Vineyard holdings include an impressive range of six top premier crus as well as four grand crus. The emphasis here is on a fairly straightforward style, with vinification and maturation largely in stainless steel for Petit Chablis, Chablis, and premier crus, and oak used only for grand crus: Les Preuses is vinified in stainless steel but partly matured in oak, and only Les Clos is both vinified and matured in barrique.

The wines are attractive and ready for drinking on release, with a citrus fruit spectrum balanced by occasional savory hints and a nice sense of texture to the palate. Servin's general style favors minerality or delicacy over power. In addition to the AOP Chablis, there is a cuvée of Vieilles Vignes from a plot of 50-year old vines in Pargues (at one time considered on a level with the premier crus Montmains and Vaillons, but abandoned during the first world war). The premier crus have more intensity than the AOP Chablis, but I do not see as much distinction between them as I would like, and although there is more intensity at the grand cru level, the only wine that strikes me as having serious aging potential is Les Clos. François also makes wines for a label under his father's name, Marcel Servin.

Maison Simonnet-Febvre ✱

CHABLIS
PREMIER CRU
VAILLONS
MILLÉSIME
2010
SIMONNET-FEBVRE
À CHABLIS

📍 9, Avenue d'Oberwesel, 89800 Chablis

📞 (33) 03 86 98 99 00

Jean-Philippe Archambaud

@ contact@simonnet-febvre.com

🌐 www.simonnet-febvre.com

🍾 Montmains

😊 🍾🍾🍾

🍇 🍾 🚜 20 ha; 800,000 bottles
[map p. 21]

"We are a bit different, because Chablis is 50%, and the rest is sparkling wine (25%) and regional wines (25%)," says Jean-Philippe Archambaud, who came to run the house after Louis Latour bought it in 2003. Simonnet-Febvre is an old house, founded in 1840, and originally concentrating on sparkling wine. Today sparkling wine is made at the old cellars just across the river from the Chablis town center, and the still wines are made in a new cellar at Chitry, a few miles away. Estate vineyards are only a small part of the supply for this large house. With 42 cuvées in all, there's a wide range of vintage and nonvintage Crémants, red and white wines from the Auxerrois, and Chablis extending from Petit Chablis to grand cru.

"Almost all our wines are made in the same way," Jean-Philippe explains: "whole bunch pressing, vinification in stainless steel, and then aging in steel on fine lees, no wood. I think most Chablis need 10-12 months aging. When we leave them on the lees we don't do racking or battonage, we just leave them alone. The Simonnet style is very much no oak, except for two grand crus, Blanchots and Les Clos, which have 15% aged in 2-year-old barriques. I'm not a fan of new oak, I don't use any even for the premier crus. The nutty impressions come from lees not oak." Petit Chablis has slightly shorter élevage at 10 months, Chablis and premier crus have 12 months, the grand crus have 17-18 months.

The Petit Chablis is fruity and workmanlike, the Chablis begins to move in a mineral direction, but there is a big jump in intensity going to the Montmains premier cru. This is the real typicity of Chablis. Vaillons is more backward, Mont de Milieu is close to grand cru intensity, and Fourchaume is richer. "Whenever I want to explain what Chablis is, I think Montmains is a good example. Our Vaillons is always a little austere, a bit flinty. Mont de Milieu is fascinating because it can be a cool year or a warm year, but you always get this exotic character, Fourchaume is lovely wine but can be richer," says Jean-Philippe. In grand crus, Preuses is tightly wound, and Les Clos has more depth but is equally backward.

Domaine Laurent Tribut ***

15 Rue de Poinchy, 89800 Chablis

(33) 03 86 42 46 22

Laurent Tribut

03 86 42 48 23

Beauroy

6.66 ha; 31,000 bottles

[map p. 20]

Laurent Tribut is married to Vincent Dauvissat's sister, Marie Clotilde, and there is a family relationship to the style of the wines. The vineyards are part of Marie Clotilde's inheritance from René Dauvissat. For the first ten years, Laurent made his wines in the Dauvissat cellars, but then he moved to his own premises in Poinchy just outside the town of Chablis. Fermentation is in stainless steel, then everything is matured in old barriques. "Everything stays six months in barrique, longer than that they would show the wood, and I don't like that," Laurent says. This small domain is a very hands-on operation—there was some difficulty in arranging an appointment because Laurent thought he might need to be in the vineyards—and the wine is made in a tiny cramped cellar stuffed with barriques.

All the wines here start out full flavored, with that distinct hint of savory character. Moving from Chablis to Lechet there is more sense of extract and greater intensity. "Léchet is Léchet," says Laurent, "it is always a bit more aggressive." Then Beauroy is a touch rounder and deeper. Montmains has the greatest intensity of the premier crus, very much the savory style with wider flavor variety, and a grip on the palate. The wines are masterful representations of their appellations.

Domaine Vrignaud

*

◎ 10, Rue De Beauvoir, 89800 Fontenay-près-Chablis

☎ (33) 03 86 42 15 69

✇ Guillaume Vrignaud

@ guillaume@domaine-vrignaud.com

⊕ www.domaine-vrignaud.com

🍾 Mont de Milieu

🚶 🍾

🚜 ⬤ 23 ha

[map p. 20]

Michel and Joëlle Vrignaud abandoned general agriculture and focused on viticulture, starting estate bottling on a small scale in 1991; a new winery was built in 2000 and extended in 2008. The domain is still in the process of making the move to bottling all its own wines, and today half of production is bottled at the domain, which is run by Michel's son, Guillaume. The domain is located in a series of buildings around a courtyard at the back of Fontenay-près-Chablis. It's a very hands-on operation, as Guillaume Vrignaud was on his tractor in the vineyards and (to the exasperation of his mother) was difficult to reach when we arrived.

The range extends from Petit Chablis and Chablis to two right bank premier crus, Fourchaume and Mont de Milieu. "We don't have any grand crus but we vinify a bit from a colleague," Joëlle Vrignaud explains. Most of the wines are vinified and aged in stainless steel, and the style shows a citric purity that develops increasing minerality and salinity moving from Petit Chablis to Chablis to Mont de Milieu.

Fourchaume is divided into three cuvées: Fourchaume *tout court*, Vaupulans. which comes from a specific plot of less than a hectare in the premier cru, and Côte de Fontenay, which comes from a hectare of older vines, more than 50 years of age. Fourchaume is sometimes aged in oak: the rich 2015 was aged in cuve, but the more acid 2014 was broadened by vinifying in wood. The old vines cuvée was vinified in cuve—"it was complex enough, it did not need oak." Fourchaume is the richest of the cuvées, and is further intensified by the concentration of the old vines.

Mini-Profiles of Important Estates

Château de Béru

32, Grande Rue, 89700 Béru
+33 03 86 75 90 43
Athénais de Béru
athenaisdeberu@gmail.com
www.chateaudeberu.com

15 ha; 65,000 bottles
[map p. 20]

The Béru family has owned the property for 400 years, but grapes went to the cooperative until Athénais de Béru took over the family property in 2006 after a career in finance. Château de Béru produces three cuvées of AOP Chablis from different plots in the vicinity, and the premier cru Vaucoupin, but the top wine, the Clos de Béru, comes from a 5 ha clos at the property. Long aging (around 18 months) takes place in a mixture of large wood casks, barriques, and amphora. The style is distinctive and can be quite herbal and saline. Negociant wines are produced under the Athénais label and include Sauvignon St. Bris and Bourgogne Rouge as well as Chablis.

Domaine Sébastien Dampt

23C Rue du Château, Milly 89800 Chablis
+33 03 86 18 96 50
Sébastien Dampt
seb.dampt@wanadoo.fr
www.sebastien-dampt.com

8.5 ha; 50,000 bottles
[map p. 20]

Domaine Daniel Dampt is the family domain, run by Daniel with his sons Vincent and Sébastien, but Vincent and Sébastien both also make wines under their own names. Sébastien started with 7 ha from the family holdings, and has purchased some further small plots. All the wines are made at the family winery in Milly (see profile of Daniel Dampt). Vinification is similar for all three domains, using stainless steel for Chablis and premier crus, although Sébastien now makes one cuvée, Les Beugnons, in a concrete egg. The style is lively and tends to minerality whichever label is used.

Domaine Agnès et Didier Dauvissat

1 Voie Gain, 89800 Beine
+33 03 86 42 46 40
Florent Dauvissat
agnes-didier.dauvissat@wanadoo.fr
domaine-dauvissat-agnes-et-didier.business.site

10 ha; 22,000 bottles   [map p. 20]

This is the most recent of the three Dauvissat domains in Chablis, created in 1987. "There were no vines in the family, so my parents had to start from scratch," says Florent Dauvissat, who came into the domain in 2011. They were able to buy some uncultivated land and plant vineyards. Today the domain has 3.5 ha in Petit Chablis, 4.5 ha of Chablis, and 2 ha of premier cru Beauroy, in the climat Côte de Savant, close to the winery. Initially the crop was sold to negociants; today half is estate-bottled, and the proportion is increasing. All the wines are vinified in stainless steel, except for a micro-cuvée of Beauroy, which ages in oak.

Clotilde Davenne

3, Rue Chantemerle, 89800 Préhy

+33 03 86 41 46 05

Clotilde Davenne

clotilde@clotidedavenne.fr

www.clotildedavenne.fr

8.5 ha; 40,000 bottles

[map p. Error! Bookmark not defined.]

Clotilde Davenne comes from a farming family, but became an oenologist. While she was working at Jean-Marc Brocard, she purchased a house in Préhy (the most southern point of the Chablis appellation) and planted some vines, selling off the grapes to help pay for the house. By 2005 she was making wine from her own domain, focused on Sauvignon Blanc from St. Bris, but with holdings in Bourgogne Blanc as well as Chablis. The estate holdings are extended by purchasing grapes from premier and grand crus. The domaine was called Les Temps Perdus, but today the wines are simply labeled as Clotilde Davenne. The style focuses on freshness, with all cuvées vinified and aged exclusively in stainless steel.

Domaine Bernard Defaix

17 Rue du Château, Milly, 89800 Chablis

+33 03 86 42 40 75

Didier Defaix

didier@bernard-defaix.com

www.bernard-defaix.com

27 ha; 300,000 bottles

[map p. 20]

This is very much a left bank domain, started by Bernard Defaix in 1959 with only 2 ha, and run since the 1990s by his sons Sylvain (winemaker) and Didier Defaix (vineyard management). The estate focuses on premier crus, which comprise about half the vineyard holdings, and its top wines are Vaillons, Les Lys (which used to be included in Vaillons but is now vinified separately), and Côte de Léchet, in which Defaix is the largest landholder. Wines are mostly aged in stainless steel. The top wine is the Reserve from old vines planted in Léchet in 1955, which is aged half in steel and half in used barriques. The range is extended into the right bank premier and grand crus by a negociant activity, labeled simply as Bernard Defaix.

Domaine Daniel-Etienne Defaix

23 Rue de Champlain, 89800 Chablis (winery)

14 Rue Auxerroise, 89800 Chablis (shop)

+33 03 86 42 14 44

Daniel Defaix

caveau@chablisdefaix.com

www.chablisdefaix.com

28 ha; 180,000 bottles

[map p. 20]

The domain claims to be the oldest in Chablis, now in its fourteenth generation under Daniel-Etienne (known as Danny), who took over from his father in 1978, and Danny's son, Paul-Etienne. Vineyards are mostly around Milly, on the left bank just west of the town of Chablis, half in Chablis and half in premier crus, and a tiny parcel in grand cru Blanchot. An unusual feature in winemaking is the extended aging, on the lees in cuve, with battonage each month. Chablis Vieilles Vignes ages for two years, and the premier crus age for four years, sometimes longer. Some premier crus from 2005 were not released until 2018. Danny Defaix says that this used to be common practice; "I'm the last of the Mohicans," he says. Three of the top wines are Vaillon (the label is singular rather than the more usual Vaillons, reflecting the fact that the Defaix plot is in the original area before the premier cru was extended), Côte de Lechet (this was considered a grand cru in the middle ages, Danny says), and Les Lys (pure Kimmeridgian terroir). Defaix has expanded into oenotourism, with a hotel and restaurant (Aux Lys de Chablis) in the center of Chablis.

Domaine Gérard Duplessis

5, Quai De Reugny, 89800 Chablis
+33 03 86 42 10 35
Lilian Duplessis
chablis-duplessis@bbox.fr
www.chablis-duplessis.com

10 ha; 25,000 bottles
[map p. 21]

Founded in 1895, the domain has been handed from father to son for five generations. Located in the heart of the town, the domain has holdings in top premier crus, with Montée de Tonnerre at the forefront. Gérard planted most of the domain, and his son Lilian Duplessis worked in Burgundy, rather than gaining experience elsewhere—"because I wanted to learn how to make Chardonnay"— before taking over in 2007. Chablis and the premier cru Vaugiraut (which has the youngest vines of the premier crus) age in stainless steel; the other premier crus age first in stainless steel followed by a further six months in old barriques. Les Clos is the only holding in the grand crus, and is fermented as well as aged in barrique. The wines can be a little tight in the first few years.

Domaine Jean Durup Père et Fils

4, Grande Rue, 89800 Maligny
+33 03 86 47 44 49
Jean-Paul Durup
contact@domainesdurup.com
www.durup-chablis.com

205 ha; 1,500,000 bottles
[map p. 20]

One of the largest producers in Chablis, Jean Durup is considered a modernist, with no use of oak, and wines on the lighter side. The family has been producing wine for a long time, but grew to its present size after 1968, when Jean Durup took over with only 2 ha. As well as expanding his own domain, Jean was involved in extending the appellation in the 1970s; today his son Jean-Paul, who claims to be the fourteenth generation, runs the domain, which includes 35 ha of premier cru but no grand crus. Wines are bottled under the names Domaine de l'Eglantière and Château de Maligny, but the cuvées are the same. The wines are well made but sometimes lack character. The top wine is the Fourchaume premier cru.

Domaine du Château de Fleys

2, rue des Fourneaux, 89800 Fleys
+33 03 86 42 47 70
Béatrice Philippon
philippon.beatrice@orange.fr
www.chablis-philippon.com

24 ha; 40,000 bottles
[map p. 20]

The domain was founded in 1868 by Julien Philippon, who acquired most of the vineyards that make up the estate today. His grandson André bought the "château" (an old hunting lodge which came with a 1 ha *clos* of vines) in 1988. André's children Béatrice and Benoît built the new cuverie, where the wine is now made, in 2006. The small level of production relative to the vineyard area reflects the fact that much of the crop is sold off. Vinification is mostly in stainless steel, but some old barriques are used also, depending on the cuvée. The top wine is the premier cru Mont de Milieu, where there is a plot of very old vines, planted in 1936.

Domaine Alain et Cyril Gautheron

18, Rue Des Prégirots, 89800 Fleys
+33 03 86 42 44 34
Alain Gautheron
vins@chablis-gautheron.com
www.chablis-gautheron.com

25 ha; 150,000 bottles
[map p. 20]

This family estate started in 1809 and is now in its sixth generation. When Alain Gautheron took over from his father in 1991, the domain was half its present size. Alain extended the vineyards and constructed a new cuverie in 2004, and in due course handed winemaking over to his son Cyril. In addition to Petit Chablis and Chablis, the domain has holdings in premier crus Vaucoupin, Mont de Milieu, Fourneaux (immediately across from the winery), and L'Homme Mort. Vinification is in stainless steel, and wine stays on the lees for 9 months. In addition to the regular cuvées, there is an organic cuvée, Emeraude Chablis, which comes from two tiny parcels.

Domaine Alain Geoffroy

4, rue de l'Equerre, 89800 Beine
+33 03 86 42 43 76
Nathalie Geoffroy
info@chablis-geoffroy.com
www.chablis-geoffroy.com

50 ha; 420,000 bottles
[map p. 20]

This family domain dates from 1850. Wines are vinified in steel or oak depending on the cuvée. Petit Chablis (from 10-year-old vines) and Chablis (from 20-40-year-old vines) are vinified in cuves of stainless steel, but the Chablis Vieilles Vignes (from 45-70-year-old vines) in oak. Premier crus, Beauroy, Vau Ligneau, and Fourchaume, are vinified in stainless steel, but the Beauroy Vieilles Vignes, and Les Clos (the sole grand cru, which comes from purchased grapes) are matured in oak. Alain has built a museum of corkscrews at the winery, with more than 5.000 examples.

Domaine Hamelin

6 route de Bleigny, 89800
Lignorelles
+33 03 86 47 54 60
Thierry Hamelin
domaine.hamelin@wanadoo.fr
www.domaine-hamelin.fr

37 ha; 270,000 bottles
[map p. 20]

Gustave Hamelin started with 2 ha of vines in 1840. With a new gravity-feed winery constructed at Lignorelles in the northwest quadrant of Chablis, Thierry Hamelin (the seventh generation in succession), together with his son Charles (who qualified in oenology and worked in New Zealand before joining his father), is now producing 10 ha of Petit Chablis, 20 ha of Chablis and Chablis Vieilles Vignes, and premier crus Beauroy and Vau-Ligneau. Vinification is exclusively in steel, and the new winery has brought increased precision to the style.

Domaine Lamblin et Fils

Rue Marguerite de Bourgogne,
89800 Maligny
+33 03 86 98 22 00
Alexandre Lamblin
infovin@lamblin.com
www.lamblin.com

7 ha; 1,000,000 bottles
[map p. 20]

The Lamblin family has been in the area for 300 years, and started producing wine under Henri Lamblin. His son Jacques developed a negociant business. Since 1987, Jacques's sons, Michel (management) and Didier (winemaking) have been in charge, joined after 2003 by their sons Clément and Alexandre. The negociant activity is well at the forefront. Chablis is about half of production; there are also wines from the Auxerrois, Burgundy, Beaujolais, and various IGPs. Chablis includes cuvées vinified in cuve and in new oak—the cuvée "Elevé en fût" was a project of the new generation—a Vieilles Vignes, five premier crus, and grand crus Vaudésir and Les Clos. The style is quite weighty.

Domaine Roland Lavantureux

4 Rue Saint-Martin, 89800 Lignorelles
+33 03 86 47 53 75
David & Arnaud Lavantureux
domaine.lavantureux@gmail.com
chablis-lavantureux.fr

21 ha; 70,000 bottles
[map p. 20]

The domain started by selling wine in casks in Auxerre and Paris; after Roland took over in 1979, he started bottling the wine, gave his name to the domain, and expanded the vineyards. He sons Arnaud and David took over in 2010. The Petit Chablis and Chablis come from around the property in Lignorelles; the Vieilles Vignes Chablis comes from some parcels of 60-year old vines in the vicinity, and Chablis Vauprin comes from a single parcel that the brothers consider to be the flagship of the domain. Premier Cru Vau de Vey comes from a 1 ha plot that is the most recent addition to the vineyards, and in grand crus there are Bougros, Vaudésir, and Fourchaume (the latter two from purchased grapes). Aging uses a mix of stainless steel and old barriques, with 20% barriques for the basic Chablis, 40% for the Vieilles Vignes and Vauprin, and moving to 100% for the grand crus, including some new oak.

Domaine des Marronniers

3, Grande Rue de Chablis, 89800 Préhy
+33 03 86 41 42 70
Laurent Ternynck
contact@chablismarronniers.com
www.chablismarronniers.com

19 ha; 135,000 bottles
[map p. 20]

Laurent et Marie-Noëlle Ternynck purchased this domain in 2013 when previous owner Bernard Legland retired. They also make wine from the Domaine de Mauperthuis, where they started in 1995 (where the range includes Bourgogne, Petit Chablis, and Chablis.) At Marroniers, Chablis and premier cru Montmains age in stainless steel; grand cru Valmur and the Valmur Vieilles Vignes (from vines planted in 1976) age in large oak casks. The Chablis can show something of the herbaceous character of their Sauvignon St. Bris.

La Meulière

18, Route de Mont de Milieu, 89800 Fleys
+33 03 86 42 13 56
Vincent Laroche
contact@chablis-meuliere.com
www.chablis-meuliere.com

24 ha; 180,000 bottles
[map p. 20]

Created by Claude Laroche in 1984, this domain comes from a branch of the Laroche family that has been involved in wine since the eighteenth century (but is not connected with the Laroche domain in Chablis). Claude's sons, Nicolas (winemaker) and Vincent, are now running the domain. There's an old cellar, used for events and tastings, but the wines are made in a newer cuverie. As a rough rule, Chablis and premier crus without description are vinified in stainless steel, while premier crus with fanciful names come from old vines and are matured in barriques or 500-liter casks, but oak maturation accounts for only about 5% of production.

68

Domaine Olivier et Alice De Moor

4 & 17 Rue Jacques Ferrand, 89800 Courgis
+33 03 86 41 47 94
Alice De Moor
aodemoor@aliceadsl.fr
www.aetodemoor.fr

10.6 ha; 45,000 bottles
[map p. 20]

Olivier and Alice de Moor planted this small domain in 1989 while they were working at other estates. They have worked full time at the domain since the first vintage in 1994. They built a small gravity-feed winery in 2007. They produce Aligoté and Sauvignon St. Bris as well as several cuvées of Chablis coming from different parcels, and some premier crus. Their Burgundian origins show in the use barrel fermentation and long aging in barriques for all wines. There's also a negociant activity called Le Vendangeur Masqué, which includes wines from other regions. Olivier argues that low-yielding, ripe Chardonnay should have a buttery, nutty character, and he views his wines as made in a sufficiently different way from the rest of Chablis that he caused something of a stir by refusing to allow them to be included in tastings from the appellation.

Maison J. Moreau et Fils

Route d'Auxerre, 89800 Chablis
+33 03 86 42 88 00
Lucie Depuydt
moreau@jmoreau-fils.com
www.jmoreau-fils.com

5,000,000 bottles
[map p. 21]

Moreau is an old negociant and grower in Chablis, and had some important vineyard holdings, but in 1997 the negociant was sold to Boisset of Burgundy, while the vineyards became the domains of Christian Moreau and Louis Moreau (see profiles). Wines are vinified in stainless style to give a mainstream style. The range includes five premier crus and three grand crus; in addition to Chablis, there are other AOPs from Burgundy and the Loire, IGPs, and Vins de France, made in a very large modern facility on the main road out of Chablis.

Domaine Moreau-Naudet

4, Chemin de la Vallée de Valvan, 89800 Chablis
+33 03 86 42 14 83
Virginie Moreau
moreau.naudet@wanadoo.fr

22.5 ha
[map p. 21]

Stéphane Moreau-Naudet and his father created the domain in 1993; setting up their winery in a house on the edge of the town. Previously they sold the grapes to negociant Regnard, and they continued to sell some grapes as they expanded the domain. Widely regarded as a very talented winemaker, Stéphane Moreau sadly died young in 2016, just after the domain moved from its headquarters in the town to new premises near Vaillons, but his wife Virginie has taken over. The policy has been to harvest late, press very slowly, and age in a mix of steel and wood, using both oval demi-muids and barriques for the wood, with a little new oak. The style tends to tautness. The range includes premier crus Forêts, Vaillons, and Montmains, and grand cru Valmur.

Domaine Sylvain Mosnier

36, Route Nationale, 89800 Beine
+33 03 86 42 43 96
Stéphanie Mosnier
sylvain.mosnier@libertysurf.fr
www.chablis-mosnier.com

18.5 ha; 55,000 bottles
[map p. 20]

The family has long been involved in producing and selling wine, and Sylvain Mosnier created the domain in 1978 when his father-in-law retired and gave him 2 ha of vines. His daughter Stéphanie gave up her career in logistics and took over when Sylvain retired in 2007. The range includes Petit Chablis, Chablis and a Vieilles Vignes, and premier crus Beauroy and Côte de Léchet, at very reasonable prices. The Vieilles Vignes Chablis is considered the flagship of the domain. Oak is used only in the Vieilles Vignes and Beauroy.

Domaine de la Motte

35, Grand Rue, 89800 Beine (shop)
35, rue du Ruisseau, 89800 Beine
(cellars)
+33 03 86 42 43 71
Bernard Michaut
caveau@chablis-michaut.fr
www.chablis-michaut.fr

28 ha; 250,000 bottles
[map p. 20]

The Michaut family has been growing vines in Beine since 1950, and the domaine was created in 2011 when they left the cooperative. Today the domain is run by Bertrand (a former chef) and his son Adrien and nephew Guillaume. Vineyards are all local, and include Petit Chablis, Chablis, a Vieilles Vignes from 40-year old vines, and premier crus Vau-Ligneau and Beauroy. Grapes are harvested by machine, and chaptalization is used. Petit Chablis, Chablis, and Val-Ligneau are aged in stainless steel; and only Beauroy sees oak.

Domaine Isabelle et Denis Pommier

31, Rue de Poinchy, 89800 Poinchy
+33 03 86 42 83 04
Isabelle Pommier
isabelle@denis-pommier.com
www.denis-pommier.com

19 ha; 130,000 bottles
[map p. 20]

Starting with 2 ha of vines in Poinchy in 1990 (with estate bottling starting in 1994), the domain has grown slowly to its present size, the latest acquisition being in premier crus Fourchaume and Beauroy in 2012. There are two cuvées each of Petit Chablis (Hauterivien is rich for the AOP) and Chablis, and four premier crus. The start of the range is aged in steel, but Chablis Croix aux Moines and the premier crus are fermented and aged one third in used barriques for 18 months. Bourgogne Pinot Noir comes from the Yonne. Because of the loss of grapes due to climatic conditions, the Grain de Survie cuvées of Bourgogne Blanc and Rouge were added from purchased grapes.

Maison Regnard

28, Boulevard du Dr Tacussel,
89800 Chablis
+33 03 86 42 10 45
Philippe Rossignol
events@deladoucette.fr
regnard-chablis.deladoucette.fr

10 ha; 500,000 bottles [map p. 21]

Dating from 1860, this negociant takes its name from founder Zéphir Regnard. It absorbed another negociant, Maison Albert Pic, in 1957, and in 1994 was purchased by the Ladoucette domain of Pouilly Fumé. The focus remains on Chablis, with all production in stainless steel. All seven grand crus are produced. Regnard is regarded as one of the best local negociants, and also produces wines from elsewhere in Burgundy.

Domaine Guy Robin et Fils

13, Rue Berthelot, 89800 Chablis
+33 03 86 42 12 63
Marie-Ange Robin
info@domaineguyrobin.com
www.domaineguyrobin.com

20 ha; 10,000 bottles
[map p. 21]

The domain goes back four generations, but made its reputation in the 1960s when Guy Robin acquired holdings of old vines, some going back to the era of phylloxera. By the turn of the century it had fallen off the charts, however, but was then revived when Marie-Ange gave up her career as a fine art dealer in Paris and returned to run the domain. The Chablis comes from 30-year old vines, while the premier and grand crus have an average age over 40 years. Chablis ages in steel, the premier crus are a roll-call of top sites, including Montée de Tonnerre, Mont de Milieu, Montmains, and Vaillons, and age in old barriques, and the top cuvees (including five of the seven grand crus) age in barriques including some new oak.

Domaine Francine et Olivier Savary

4, Chemin des Hâtes, 89800 Maligny
+33 03 86 47 42 09
Olivier Savary
contact@chablis-savary.com
www.chablis-savary.com

20 ha; 200,000 bottles [map p. 20]

Olivier Savary comes from a winemaking family, but did not inherit any vineyards. After attending oenology school in Dijon, he started out with his wife Francine by renting vineyards. Initially most of the crop was sold, but by 1990 the Savarys were bottling under their own label, and this has now become a well-regarded small family estate. Their sons Maxime and Mathieu are now involved. Wines include Chablis (blended from plots throughout the AOP), Vieilles Vignes, premier crus Vaillons and Fourchaumes, and grand cru Preuses. Chablis and Vaillons are aged in steel, Fourchaumes and Preuses in old barriques.

Domaine Testut

38, Rue des Moulins, 89800 Chablis
+33 03 86 42 17 50 / +33 03 86 42 45 00
Cyril Testut
cyriltestut@orange.fr
www.domaine-testut.fr

13 ha; 90,000 bottles
[map p. 21]

Philippe Testut started making Chablis in 1967, and bought vineyards. but due to family difficulties many were later sold off. Philippe went off to Châteauneuf-du-Pape, but came back to help when his son Cyril took over in 1998 and resumed estate bottling. Chablis Rive Droite is a blend exclusively from the right bank, and there are three top premier crus, Fôrets, Vaillons, and Montée de Tonnerre, and grand cru Grenouilles (a rarity that owes its inclusion to the fact that Philippe Testut came from Grenouilles). Grenouilles is the only cuvée to see any oak. Vines are over 40-years-old for Chablis, and over 50-years-old for the crus.

Domaine de La Tour

3, Route de Monfort, 89800 Lignorelles, Chablis
+33 03 86 47 55 68
Vincent Fabrici
contact@ledomainedelatour.info
www.ledomainedelatour.eu

14 ha; 25,000 bottles [map p. 20]

The Domaine de la Tour acquired its present name when Jacques Chalmeau (whose family had been making wine in the area for two hundred years) handed over in 1992 to his son-in-law, Renato Fabrici (who was Italian by origin). This remains a small family domain, and Renato's son, Vincent, is now in charge. Petit Chablis, Chablis, and two less-known premier crus, are vinified in cuve; premier cru Montmains is aged in a mix of vats and oak. The Chablis and Montmains together are the majority of production. There are also Bourgogne Blanc and Aligoté.

Domaine Gérard Tremblay

12, Rue de Poinchy, 89800 Chablis
+33 03 86 42 40 98
Vincent Tremblay
contact@chablis-tremblay.com
www.chablis-tremblay.com

37 ha; 250,000 bottles
[map p. 20]

Now led by the fifth generation, the domain has tripled in size since Gérard took over in 1970 and started estate-bottling. At first wine was sold only at the cellar door; now it is exported worldwide. A gravity-feed winery was constructed in 1990. A third of the estate is in premier or grand cru. Gérard's son Vincent worked in Australia, and has been at the domain since 1999. In addition to Petit Chablis and Chablis (aged in cuve), there are two cuvées of Vieilles Vignes from 40-year old vines. One is aged in steel; Cuvée Hélène comes from the same juice, but is aged in new oak. Premier cru Fourchaume (the only right bank cru of the domain) is aged in steel, but the other premier crus, and grand cru Vaudésir, are aged in a mix of steel and old barriques.

Domaine Vocoret et Fils

40, Route d'Auxerre, 89800 Chablis
+33 03 86 42 12 53
Patrice & Jérôme Vocoret
contact@domainevocoret.com
www.domaine-vocoret.com

50 ha; 300,000 bottles
[map p. 21]

Founded by Edouard Vocoret in 1870, this is one of the larger domains in Chablis, now managed by Patrice (winemaker) and his nephew Jérome (viticulturalist). The domain has been bottling its own wines since 1930. The village wine is aged in steel, but Vocoret is known for its forceful style, running through an impressive range of the best premier crus and four grand crus, all matured in old oak foudres; close to half the vineyards are premier or grand cru. Some of the top wines get greater oak exposure in the form of demi-muids.

Maison Verget

Le Bourg, 71960 Sologny
+33 03 85 51 66 00
Jean-Marie Guffens
contact@verget-sa.com
www.verget-sa.fr

0 ha; 360,000 bottles

Jean-Marie Guffens was twenty or thirty years ahead of his time when he started making Chablis in a rich style more resembling the Côte d'Or than the acid wines of the era. As a negociant without land holdings, his cuvées may vary from year to year, but the Chablis is always flavorful, premier crus have depth, and grand crus have increased concentration. Verget produces wines from all over Burgundy, always in the same characterful style (see profile in *Guide to Southern Burgundy*).

Domaine Eleni et Édouard Vocoret

19, rue de Chichée, 89800 Chablis
+33 09 53 21 66 20
Eleni & Édouard Vocoret
info@vocoret.fr
www.vocoret.fr

5 ha
[map p. 21]

Edouard's family owns Domaine Vocoret, and he founded this small domain in 2016 together with his wife Eléni, whom he met while working the harvest in New Zealand. The vineyards came from the family holdings. There are two wines: Chablis Bas le Chapelot comes from just below Montée de Tonnerre, and premier cru Les Butteaux comes from a tiny parcel in Montée de Tonnerre. The wines ferment in steel, and then age in old barriques, 9 months for the village wine, and 12 months for the premier cru.

Glossary of French Wine Terms

Classification

There are three levels of classification, but their names have changed:

- *AOP* (Appellation d'Origine Protégée, formerly AOC or Appellation d'Origine Contrôlée) is the highest level of classification. AOPs are tightly regulated for which grape varieties can be planted and for various aspects of viticulture and vinification.
- *IGP* (Indication Géographique Protegée, formerly Vin de Pays) covers broader areas with more flexibility for planting grape varieties, and few or no restrictions on viticulture and vinification.
- *Vin de France* (formerly Vin de Table) is the lowest level of classification and allows complete freedom with regards to varieties, viticulture, and vinification.
- *INAO* is the regulatory authority for AOP and IGP wines.

Producers

- *Domaine* on a label means the wine is produced only from estate grapes (the vineyards may be owned or rented).
- *Maison* on the label means that the producer is a negociant who has purchased grapes (or wine).
- *Negociants* may purchase grapes and make wine or may purchase wine in bulk for bottling themselves. Some negociants also own vineyards.
- *Cooperatives* buy the grapes from their members and make the wine to sell under their own label.

Growers

- There is no word for winemaker in French. The closest would be *oenologue*, meaning a specialist in vinification; larger estates (especially in Bordeaux) may have consulting oenologues.
- A *vigneron* is a wine grower, who both grows grapes and makes wine.
- A *viticulteur* grows grapes but does not make wine.
- A *régisseur* is the estate manager at a larger property, and may encompass anything from general management to taking charge of viticulture or (commonly) vinification.

Viticulture

- There are three types of viticulture where use of conventional treatments (herbicides, insecticides, fertilizers, etc.) is restricted:
- *Bio* is organic viticulture; certification is by AB France (Agriculture Biologique).
- *Biodynamique* is biodynamic viticulture, certified by Demeter.
- *Lutte raisonnée* means sustainable viticulture (using treatments only when necessary). There are various certifications including HVE (Haute Valeur Environmentale).

- *Selection Massale* means that cuttings are taken from the best grape-vines in a vineyard and then grafted on to rootstocks in order to replant the vineyard.
- *Clonal selection* uses (commercially available) clones to replant a vineyard.
- *Vendange Vert* (green pruning) removes some berries during the season to reduce the yield.

Winemaking

- *Vendange entière* means that whole clusters of grapes are used for fermentation.
- *Destemming* means that the grapes are taken off the stems and individual berries are put into the fermentation vat.
- During fermentation of red wine, grape skins are pushed up to the surface to form a cap. There are three ways of dealing with it:
  - *Pigeage* (*Punch-down*) means using a plunger to push the cap into the fermenting wine.
  - *Remontage* (pump-over) means pumping up the fermenting wine from the bottom of the vat to spray over the cap.
  - *Délestage* (rack-and-return) means running the juice completely out of the tank, and then pouring it over the cap (which has fallen to the bottom of the vat)
- *Chaptalization* is the addition of sugar before or during fermentation. The sugar is converted into alcohol, so the result is to strengthen the alcoholic level of the wine, not to sweeten it.
- A *cuve* is a large vat of neutral material—old wood, concrete, or stainless steel.
- *Cuvaison* is the period a wine spends in contact with the grape skins.
- *Battonage* describes stirring up the wine when it is aging (usually) in cask.
- *Soutirage* (racking) transfers the wine (without the lees) from one barrique to another.
- *Élevage* is the aging of wine after fermentation has been completed.
- *Malo* is an abbreviation for malolactic fermentation, performed after the alcoholic fermentation, which reduces acidity. It's almost always done with red wines, and most often for non-aromatic white wines.
- A *vin de garde* is a wine intended for long aging.

Aging in oak

- A *fût* (*de chêne*) is an oak barrel of unspecified size.
- A *barrique* (in Bordeaux or elsewhere) has 225 liters or 228 liters (called a *pièce* in Burgundy).
- A *tonneau* is an old term for a 900 liter container, sometimes used colloquially for containers larger than barriques, most often 500 or 600 liter.
- A *demi-muid* is a 600 liter barrel.
- A *foudre* is a large oak cask, round or oval, from 20-100 hl.

Index of Estates by Rating

4 star
Domaine Vincent Dauvissat
Domaine François Raveneau
3 star
Domaine Louis Michel
Domaine Laurent Tribut
2 star
Domaine Jean-Claude et Romain Bessin
Domaine Samuel Billaud
Domaine Billaud Simon
Domaine Jean-Paul et Benoît Droin
Domaine William Fèvre
Domaine Laroche
Domaine Christian Moreau Père et Fils
1 star
Jean-Marc Brocard
La Chablisienne
Domaine de Chantemerle
Jean Collet et Fils
Domaine Daniel Dampt et fils
Jean et Sébastien Dauvissat
Domaine Drouhin-Vaudon
Domaine Nathalie et Gilles Fèvre
Domaine Garnier et Fils
Domaine Guilhem & Jean-Hugues Goisot
Domaine Jean-Pierre et Corinne Grossot
Domaine Long-Depaquit
Domaine des Malandes
La Manufacture
Domaine Louis Moreau
Domaine Pattes Loup
Domaine Gilbert Picq et Fils
Domaine Pinson Frères
Patrick Piuze
L & C Poitout
Domaine Denis Race
Domaine Servin
Maison Simonnet-Febvre
Domaine Vrignaud

Index of Organic and Biodynamic Estates

Château de Béru
Jean-Marc Brocard
Domaine Vincent Dauvissat
Domaine Bernard Defaix
Domaine Drouhin-Vaudon
Domaine Gérard Duplessis
Domaine William Fèvre
Domaine Guilhem & Jean-Hugues Goisot
Domaine Jean-Pierre et Corinne Grossot
Domaine Laroche
Domaine Olivier et Alice De Moor
Domaine Christian Moreau Père et Fils
Domaine Pattes Loup
Domaine Isabelle et Denis Pommier

Index of Estates by Name

Château de Béru, 63
Domaine Jean-Claude et Romain Bessin, 23
Domaine Samuel Billaud, 15, 24
Domaine Billaud Simon, 15, 25
Jean-Marc Brocard, 26
La Chablisienne, 15, 28
Domaine de Chantemerle, 29
Jean Collet et Fils, 15, 30
Domaine Daniel Dampt et fils, 31
Domaine Sébastien Dampt, 63
Domaine Agnès et Didier Dauvissat, 63
Jean et Sébastien Dauvissat, 33
Domaine Vincent Dauvissat, 15, 34
Clotilde Davenne, 64
Domaine Bernard Defaix, 64
Domaine Daniel-Etienne Defaix, 64
Domaine Jean-Paul et Benoît Droin, 15, 15, 35
Domaine Drouhin-Vaudon, 36
Domaine Gérard Duplessis, 65
Domaine Jean Durup Père et Fils, 65
Domaine Nathalie et Gilles Fèvre, 37
Domaine William Fèvre 15, 38
Domaine du Château de Fleys, 65
Domaine Garnier et Fils, 39
Domaine Alain et Cyril Gautheron, 66
Domaine Alain Geoffroy, 66
Domaine Guilhem & Jean-Hugues Goisot, 40
Domaine Jean-Pierre et Corinne Grossot, 41
Domaine Hamelin, 66
Domaine Lamblin et Fils, 66
Domaine Laroche, 15, 42
Domaine Roland Lavantureux, 67
Domaine Long-Depaquit, 43

Domaine des Malandes, 44
La Manufacture, 15, 46
Domaine des Marronniers, 67
La Meulière, 67
Domaine Louis Michel, 15, 47
Domaine Olivier et Alice De Moor, 68
Maison J. Moreau et Fils, 68
Domaine Christian Moreau Père et Fils, 49
Domaine Louis Moreau, 15, 50
Domaine Moreau-Naudet, 68
Domaine Sylvain Mosnier, 69
Domaine de la Motte, 69
Domaine Pattes Loup, 51
Domaine Gilbert Picq et Fils, 52
Domaine Pinson Frères, 53
Patrick Piuze, 54
L & C Poitout, 55
Domaine Isabelle et Denis Pommier, 69
Domaine Denis Race, 57
Domaine François Raveneau, 15, 58
Maison Regnard, 69
Domaine Guy Robin et Fils, 70
Domaine Francine et Olivier Savary, 70
Domaine Servin, 59
Maison Simonnet-Febvre, 60
Domaine Testut, 70
Domaine de La Tour, 70
Domaine Gérard Tremblay, 71
Domaine Laurent Tribut, 15, 61
Maison Verget, 71
Domaine Vocoret et Fils, 71
Domaine Eleni et Édouard Vocoret, 71
Domaine Vrignaud, 15, 62

Made in the USA
Monee, IL
10 August 2020